Espresso for Your Spirit

Espresso for your Spirit

Hope and Humor for Pooped Out Parents

PAM VREDEVELT

Multnomah Publishers® Sisters, Oregon

ESPRESSO FOR YOUR SPIRIT
Hope and Humor for Pooped-Out Parents
published by Multnomah Publishers, Inc.

© 1999 by Pam Vredevelt
International Standard Book Number 1-57673-485-4

Design by Mark Mickel
Cover art by Michael Crompton/Mendola Ltd.

Most Scripture quotations are taken from:
The Holy Bible, New International Version (NIV) © 1973, 1984 by International Bible Society.
Used by permission of Zondervan Publishing House.

Also quoted: *The Message* © 1993 by Eugene H. Peterson
The Living Bible (TLB) © 1971 by Tyndale House Publishers, Inc.
The Holy Bible, New King James Version (NKJV) © 1984 by Thomas Nelson, Inc.
Used by permission. All rights reserved.

The Holy Bible, New Living Translation (NLT), © 1996. Used by permission of
Tyndale House Publishers, Inc. All rights reserved.

New American Standard Bible (NASB) 1960, 1977 by the Lockman Foundation
The New Testament in Modern English, Revised Edition (Phillips) © 1958, 1960, 1972 by J. B. Phillips

Printed in the United States

For information:
MULTNOMAH PUBLISHERS, INC.
Post Office Box 1720
Sisters, Oregon 97759

Library of Congress Cataloging-in-Publication Data

Vredevelt, Pam W., 1955–
Espresso for your spirit: hope and humor for pooped-out parents
/ by Pam Vredevelt.
p. cm.
ISBN 1–57673–485–4 (alk. paper)
1. Parenting. 2. Parenting—Religious aspects—Christianity.
I. Title.
HQ755.8.V74 1999
248.8′ 45—dc21
99–15627
CIP

99 00 01 02 03 04 05 06—10 9 8 7 6 5 4 3 2 1

To my parents and parents-in-law,

Chuck and Dana,
and
John and Doris,

for their sacrificial love and their knack for helping John
and me see the lighter side of life,
especially when we're pooped out.

Contents

Acknowledgments

A year ago, John and I sat in a conference room at Multnomah Publishers headquarters with Don Jacobson and his leadership team. We brainstormed ideas, talked about five-year goals, and dreamed about launching a series of books entitled *Espresso for Your Spirit*. The first book, which you hold in your hands, is complete thanks to the investment of many talented people.

I want to thank Don and Brenda Jacobson for their vision and belief in me as a writer. Your encouragement has given me a turbocharged boost to keep the coffeepot hot and the ideas flowing.

I also want to thank Keith Wall for his skillful editing. He has scoured the cup clean and added just the right amount of cream and sugar to make *Espresso* a delightful brew.

Chris Sundquist, Michele Tennesen, Steve Shepherd, Jeff Pederson, Steve Curley, and Kevin Marks—you have all been an encouragement to me as I've faced the daily grind of developing one story at a time. Thank you for your creative expertise, marketing vision, and enthusiasm for delivering cup after cup of inspiration to pooped-out moms and dads.

Thanks also to the moms and dads who have been gracious enough to tell their stories in this book. Your testimonies reflect God's never-ending faithfulness in the midst of life's hard realities. I am certain that many a weary soul will find fresh hope in what you have shared.

Then there are my treasured friends who have spurred me on. To all those who have prayed for me, walked with me, and encouraged me chapter after chapter...Let's plan a party!

And last, but certainly not least, I want to thank John, my partner in life, for hanging tough with me in the more difficult seasons of parenting. I'm grateful for your love and uncompromising faithfulness to me and the children. You and I are not perfect parents, and we never will be. But by God's grace, we'll keep making improvements. I'm certain God will continue to use Jessie, Ben, and Nathan—His greatest gifts to us—to reveal our deep need for Him and His life-changing power in our family.

INTRODUCTION

The Coffee's Brewing

I finished dunking my tea bag for the last time, tossed it in the wastebasket and then asked my next counseling client to join me in my office. She bounced into the room and plopped down on the couch.

Noticing my teacup she said, "So, you like the lightweight stuff, eh? If you want a real boost, you should try mine." With a grin and an energetic toast, she extolled, "A triple espresso will cure what ails you every time!"

I chuckled and wondered why we were doing therapy.

I have to admit, I like the stuff, too. Well, maybe not a *triple* espresso. My neurons can't handle that kind of a jolt, but I do enjoy a piping-hot, fresh-ground latté with whipped cream and chocolate sprinkles. One of the doctors I work with tends to be healthier in his dietary selections and usually ribs me when I bring a latté to the office.

"So, Pam, are you mood altering again?" he asks with a playful smirk.

I dish it back: "You bet, and in fifteen minutes you're going to be glad I did. I drink coffee for your protection, you know." A lip-smacking latté tends to clear out mental cobwebs and sweep away the grouchies.

A walking partner of mine recently asked, "Pam, what's your newest book about?"

"Well," I pondered, "it's for moms and dads who want to mood-alter. Do you think my conservative friends will go for it?" As a former druggie, she loved the concept.

"Actually, I'm writing it for myself," I continued. "It's for my bedside table, or the coffee table in the living room....

• Something I can pick up for a few minutes in the morning with a fresh cup of coffee.

• Something to alter my mood when I'm pooped out and discouraged.

- Something to give me a lift at the end of a long hard day.
- Something to help me shift gears from feeling harried to feeling hopeful."

It's definitely not a clinical guide that details what we should or shouldn't do as parents. God knows (and so do our kids) that my husband, John, and I are not experts in the field. We try hard to be good parents, but many times we fall short of our ideals.

At 10:00 P.M., after long work hours, nine loads of laundry, a pile of dirty diapers, fifteen snotty Kleenex's, bouts with adolescent attitudes, and endless rapid-fire questions and requests, I don't need instruction about "how to do it right"…which would only remind me how I'm doing it wrong. I need some espresso for my spirit. Make it a triple. Premium leaded. The kind that will prop a spoon straight up.

Let's face it, being a parent is hard work. It demands years of blood, sweat, and tears, which sculpt lines in our faces and turn our hair colors we spend paychecks covering up. Most moms and dads begin parenting feeling somewhat fit and well proportioned. But when we compare our before and after pictures, everything in the latter appears saggy, droopy, and haggard. You know you're a seasoned parent when you find relief when you scrutinize the unclad natives in *National Geographic* and think, *I'm not so bad after all.*

But the physical changes we endure aren't really the biggest challenge. Most parents have a much harder time dealing with the emotional issues that emerge during parenting, such as:

- The fear evoked by the unfamiliar.
- The guilt that bogs us down over obvious mistakes.
- The anger that erupts when crossed by a child's unrelenting, cast-iron will.
- The disappointment that comes from seeing a child make unhealthy choices.
- The inadequacy that surfaces when we slow down long enough to face ourselves.
- The grief we feel when letting go of some of our dreams, our

expectations, and then our children as they grow up and move on.

There is nothing easy about any of this.

When someone suggested I write a book for parents, I laughed and said, "You're asking the wrong person. John and I are still trying to figure out how to parent our own kids. I don't know 'Twelve Easy Steps to Confident Parenting.' We're still in the trenches, blowing bubbles in the mud. I think you need someone who is on the other side of parenting, whose kids are grown and gone."

The person disagreed for various reasons and then popped the question, "If you had a gift you could give to other parents, what would it be?"

My answer was immediate: "Hope and humor!" Two things I knew I needed in daily doses.

I remember one evening when I was filled with anxiety over our little boy Nathan, who has Down Syndrome. He had suffered several recurring illnesses, and we were still waiting to hear whether or not he would need open-heart surgery. There's no denying it, I was extremely worried. And I was packing around a burden of guilt over my inability to give my husband and our older children, Jessie and Ben, the same amount of attention I had before Nathan arrived. I unloaded on one of my friends who prayed for me in a way I will never forget: "God, Pam is weary to the bone. Stand up tall inside her. Bolster her. Infuse her with Your strength." And after she closed with an "Amen," she offered words of encouragement born out of her own struggles.

Something changed that night. God energized me through a thoughtful prayer and a few well-chosen words. Outside, things were the same. But inside, I was different. The clinician in me said, "Now that was a powerful intervention."

I thought about all the parents with whom I've had the privilege of spending time in the counseling office. The depressed. The anxious. The traumatized. The grieving. The broken. The terminally ill. The conflicted. The burned out. The betrayed. The abandoned. All the moms and dads who needed to know they were not alone in their journey.

Espresso for Your Spirit is for those of you who are in the trenches trying your best to be a decent parent and to love your kids. You're giving 110 percent and every now and then you feel you're in over your head. You're pooped out, stressed out, and need a fifteen-minute break to reconnect yourself with your Creator. Perhaps you've had thoughts similar to mine: *God, this assignment is too big for me. I don't think I'm up to the task.*

If you have drawn that conclusion, you are right where you need to be. We were never designed to parent solo. We need outside help. The good news is, we can tap into God's power, and He can accomplish what we can't.

As you "drink in" the pages that follow, I hope your spirit will be energized and that you'll split a gut over the funny quips. Laugh. Cry. Be filled with cup after cup of hope and humor as you meet real people whom God has intercepted in moving and compelling ways. And know that God is orchestrating His plans in you and in your children. He is at your side. Take courage! Everything isn't all up to you.

Espresso for Your Spirit is designed for individual reading as well as small-group discussion. In the back of the book are "Koffee Klatch Questions" for those who want to discuss the joys and challenges of parenting with other moms and dads over a cup of coffee. The questions will encourage you to think in terms of concrete parenting goals. If it suits your fancy, put on the coffeepot and invite a few friends to enjoy some hope and humor along with you.

By the way, after a triple shot of this espresso, there are no caffeine buzzes or crash landings. The piles of fluffy whipped cream have no calories, and the melt-in-your-mouth chocolate accents won't rot your teeth. So forget about self-control and imbibe to your heart's content. I do hope each sip of a chapter gives your spirit a turbocharged perk that leaves you craving more.

With a hug for your journey,

Pam Vredevelt

ESPRESSO LINGO:
What's Your Fancy?

ESPRESSO is an Italian word that means "express" or fast, which is related to the speedy way espresso is made. "Express" also refers to a substance that has been pressed and served by the cup "expressly" for one person.

CAFÉ ESPRESSO is one shot of espresso served in a small, two-ounce cup to be consumed in one swallow. Especially for those with cast-iron stomachs.

CAFÉ MACCHIATO is espresso served in an espresso cup and topped off with a dollop of foamed milk.

CAFÉ LATTÉ consists of one, two, or three shots of espresso in a tall cup filled with steamed milk, topped with foam and flavorful sprinkles if desired. My favorite.

CAPPUCCINO is a beverage containing one-third espresso, one-third steamed milk, and one-third foam.

GRANITA has the consistency of an iced smoothie and is made with frozen, diluted, sweetened espresso.

* * * *

A CYNIC'S DEFINITION OF ESPRESSO: A mud-brown beverage consisting of dry, crushed tropical beans methodically blasted with scalding water and consumed in massive quantities for its power to produce a satisfactory level of nervous agitation. (Such a gloomy way to look at life, don't you think?)

CHAPTER 1

Time for a Refill

$\mathcal{D}$o not be surprised at the painful trial you are suffering, as though something strange were happening to you. But rejoice that you participate in the sufferings of Christ."

—1 Peter 4:12–13

I have been working as a therapist for nearly twenty years, and I've met scores of suffering parents. I've seen many tears and passed hundreds of boxes of Kleenex. I think of all the mothers of preschoolers I've talked with who were discouraged and depressed. They constantly poured out energy and effort, with little opportunity to refill their cup. No immediate rewards were given to them. The children certainly were not patting them on the back, saying, "Way to go, Mom! You're doing a great job!"

When we take on the assignment of parenting, most of us don't have a clue what we are doing. It's like trying to drive through a thick blanket of San Francisco fog, where we can see only a few inches in front of us. It's downright scary. Then, by the time we've got a few things figured out, we've worked ourselves out of a job.

Last year, John and I decided to attend a support group for moms and dads called "Parenting like the Father." We wanted to gather some more tools for guiding our three children more effectively. When we walked in, several people greeted us with a startled expression and asked, "What are you doing here?"

"We're here for the parenting class," we answered.

"You are?" they exclaimed.

Between the lines what they were really saying was, "I thought pastors and therapists had their act together and already knew all this stuff." It didn't take them long to figure out we, too, had our moments of floundering! We spoke candidly about Nathan's escapes and our hair-raising searches for him throughout the neighborhood. (Now, every door in the house is secured with latches beyond his reach.) We also shared the challenges of parenting three children whose uniquenesses necessitate different parenting styles. Two are strong willed; one is compliant. Two are talented and gifted; one is mentally and physically challenged. Strategies that are effective with one can backfire with another. Sometimes John and I look at each other with baffled expressions, wondering how this thing called family is supposed to work.

The group met for ten weeks, and we were amazed at the strength we drew from those times together. No one doled out magic formulas. No one played the expert. Those attending courageously discussed their "trouble spots." We brainstormed strategies. We set weekly goals. We kept each other accountable. Sometimes we puzzled over problems that didn't have cut-and-dried solutions—but we found hope and healing simply in voicing our concerns in a safe and reassuring context.

Today, some of our old trouble spots no longer exist in our home. Other problem areas have improved. And, of course, some things remain a struggle. But that's how it is when all five members of our household are still in process.

It occurs to me that there is a certain group of parents that suffer more than others, regardless of their children's issues. They are those who spend much of their energy trying to make the family look good on the outside, without openly addressing problems inside the family.

When we pretend things are fine, and they aren't, we all suffer. When we close dialogue on conflicts, we perpetuate pain. Denial often leads to some form of relational death.

I view this as unnecessary suffering, the same as a diabetic failing to take insulin or a clinically depressed person refusing medication. We have the power to make healthy choices. We don't have to deny that issues exist. We can accept family problems as a natural part of life, face them squarely, and make necessary adjustments for the sake of the clan.

I remember one mom who was asked, "If you had it to do over again, would you have children?"

Without skipping a beat, she said, "Oh yes! Just not the same ones!"

Behind closed doors, another mom confessed, "Nobody told me parenting was going to be this hard. I'm not sure I would have had kids if I'd known six years ago what I know today. My kids bring out the worst in me. I feel like a mean old nag. I yell. I snap. And there's never any time to do what I want to do. Somewhere along the way I lost myself."

Granted, this mom's life was out of balance. She desperately needed help setting boundaries and forming realistic expectations about her four active little ones. But her comment about losing herself struck a chord in me.

I remember the months following our little Nathan's traumatic entry into this world. He arrived six weeks early with a diagnosis of severe heart complications and Down Syndrome. I was completely overwhelmed by the thought of meeting the rest of my family's needs with the addition of a mentally retarded child. There simply wasn't enough of me to go around, a feeling most parents have experienced when their cup was emptied into busy schedules, time pressures, and other chronic stresses.

Two months after we brought Nathan home from the hospital, I stood in the shower telling God all about it.

"I am so sick of crying, God," I said. "I've cried every day for the last two months, and I'm sick of it. I can't fix me. I can't fix my family. I can't fix Nathan. God, I need help."

I call that ten-minute episode my "Surrender in the Shower." It was a turning point for me.

I surrendered to the fact that I was powerless to change Nathan's condition. I couldn't rewrite the script, nor could I erase the previous year of my life.

I surrendered to the fact that I wasn't capable of meeting my children's needs in the way that I wanted. God knew that, too, and He was going to have to make up the difference.

I surrendered to the realization that I couldn't control the future. It was in God's hands.

And I surrendered to the fact that my feelings were my feelings—even though I hated them—and the only way to get beyond the grief was to go through it and to trust that in God's perfect time He would heal my heart.

That act of surrender eased my pain. I understood that Nathan's issues were beyond me and that the healing I longed for in our family was beyond me, too.

When we become parents, part of us is lost. But it's not necessarily a bad loss. Parenting chips away at any orientation toward self.

It forces us to be more other-centered. It necessitates laying down our lives. It requires an emptying of who we are for the sake of those who follow.

I used to think raising children was more or less a task of shaping and guiding a future generation. I still do. But I also think God uses children to shape parents. And the trials that come into our family circle aren't necessarily to make us "better." They are to "empty us out" so that God can fill us up with more of Himself.

I wonder if Jesus had this in mind when He said, "You will drink the cup I drink" (Mark 10:39).

Power Perk: A SIP OF HUMOR

"Nothing stops a family quarrel more quickly than the arrival of an unexpected guest."[1]

One time, Sir Winston Churchill and Lady Astor were discussing the role of women in Parliament, something he opposed and she championed. Frustrated with the conversation, Lady Astor said in exasperation, "Sir Winston, if I were your wife, I would put arsenic in your coffee."

"Madam," Churchill replied, "if I were your husband, I'd drink it."

A Chinese proverb says: Nobody's family can hang out the sign, Nothing the Matter Here.[2]

CHAPTER 2

Angel Sightings

*W*atch what God does, and then you do it, like children who learn proper behavior from their parents. Mostly what God does is love you. Keep company with him and learn a life of love. Observe how Christ loved us. His love was not cautious but extravagant. He didn't love in order to get something from us but to give everything of himself to us. Love like that."

—Ephesians 5:1–2, *The Message*

If you have read my book *Angel Behind the Rocking Chair: Stories of Hope in Unexpected Places,* you know about the angel sightings in our home. Nathan, our little boy who has Down Syndrome, tells us with sign language whenever he observes an angel nearby.

The first incident happened when he was eighteen months old. I was feeding him with a bottle while rocking him in the big stuffed rocker in the nursery. It was a typical night, and we were carrying out our usual bedtime routine. But rather than looking at me while I fed him, he kept turning his head toward the blank wall on the opposite side of the room. It was dark, and for the life of me I couldn't see anything there to distract him or hold his attention.

I kept turning Nathan's head back toward me, but after the

fourth time, I knew it would be no use. His sights were locked on to something. But there was nothing there. No shadow, no pattern of light. Nothing.

By then I was becoming curious. "Nathan," I said softly, "do you see something? What do you see?"

I'm not sure what prompted me, but I turned his head toward me again and said, "Nathan, do you see angels?"

I still don't know why I asked that question because angels weren't a topic of conversation in our home. But when I used the word, I could tell from Nathan's body language that he knew what I meant.

He riveted his attention back on the blank wall and smiled from ear to ear. It was as if he were saying, "Way to go, Mom. You finally got it."

I hid that incident in my heart and told only John about it. I suppose part of me doubted that Nathan actually saw an angel. As a therapist, I know the power of suggestion, and I wondered if I had simply planted the thought in his mind.

Then something out of the ordinary happened again when he was three years old. The scene was much the same. Same rocker. Same nightly ritual. By this time he was bigger and rather than lying in my arms, he tucked his knees up in my lap and rested his head on my shoulder while I sang. When we were both nearly asleep, he bolted straight back, bounced up and down, and pointed wildly behind the rocker, shouting, "Aaa! Aaa! Aaa!"

Impatient with his antics, I retorted, "Nathan, it is not time to play! It is time to sleep!"

But he kept bouncing, pointing behind the chair, and shouting, "Aaa! Aaa! Aaa!"

His persistence suddenly reminded me of that earlier time when he'd stared and smiled at the wall.

"Nathan," I asked, "do you see angels?"

This time he added "Da!" to his smile, put his head back down, and promptly fell asleep. "Da" in Nathan's vocabulary means "yes."

Being a doubting Thomas, I ran a test the next morning. When our friend Margaret came to the house, I said, "Nathan, can you show Margaret where you saw the angels last night?"

He took her by the hand, marched her down the hall to the nursery, and pointed behind the rocker. I was no longer a skeptic.

Another sighting occurred on one of those bleak days when everything seems gray and miserable. Our whole family stayed home from church that Sunday morning because John and Nathan had the flu. Everyone was grumpy and out of sorts. In the midst of the chaos, Nathan bolted into the kitchen with shining eyes.

"Mama! Mama!" he said urgently.

When I looked at him, he tapped his shoulders with his hands and made a flapping motion out to the side, like children do when they pretend to fly.

"Nathan," I said slowly, "do you see an angel?"

He nodded vigorously and pointed past Ben and me, through the doorway between the kitchen and the living room. His eyes were fixed on something, and he knew he wanted us to see what he saw.

"Do you see an angel in the living room?"

A sparkly smile lit up his face, and he bobbed his head.

"Well, Nathan," I said with a sigh, "we could certainly use an angel or two in this house today."

More than eight months had passed since the last time Nathan had told us he had seen an angel. We hadn't been talking about angels that morning, and Nathan simply does not possess the cognitive skills to fabricate reality.

For me, the timing of this particular angel (or angels) was significant.

We were all quarrelsome and surly, muttering negative comments and lobbing verbal hand grenades at one another. We had skipped church. Some of us were sick. And I felt more discouraged than I had in a long time. Frankly, our home didn't seem a very likely place for an angelic visitation. It was easier for me to picture an angel dropping in on Billy Graham's family or peeking in on the church service we had missed. Surely, the angel would rather be somewhere more "godly" than the Vredevelt's battlefield.

But God wanted to remind us that He was with us...

In the midst of chaos...

In the midst of our imperfection...

In the midst of our angry words...

In the midst of our jangled nerves...

In the midst of my pity party.

On a dark winter morning, on a day that seemed anything but divine, in an atmosphere that seemed none too heavenly, God dispatched a representative. And the only one who had eyes to see was a little observer with Down Syndrome.[1]

The grace and love God extended to five "unlovely" people that morning overwhelms me to this day. It seems to be a theme He continues to weave through our family experiences in creative ways.

We were en route from Portland to Nashville for a big family reunion. All the flights were overbooked, and we barely made our connection in Chicago. When we reached the ticket counter, the agent told us we wouldn't be able to sit together. Nathan and I had the only two seats left together, while John, Jessie, and Ben were squeezed in wherever. We boarded the plane, and the doors immediately closed behind us.

Nathan and I hurried as quickly as we could to our assigned seats. (No small task lugging a diaper bag, purse, umbrella stroller, and Nathan's Winnie-the-Pooh backpack full of books and a cassette tape player.) When we stopped at our row, there, sitting next to the window, was a woman in full business attire. Black suit. White collar. Briefcase to match. Very professional. I think she was probably counting on having two vacant seats next to her since the plane was just about to leave the gate before we boarded. When she saw us, she was not a happy camper.

With a sneer, she said, "Oh, blankety, blank, blank!" (Pam's paraphrase).

Well, great! I thought. *It's going to be a very long flight!*

In all fairness to our traveling companion, I remember times when I've flown on business, and the last thing I wanted was a crying baby or rambunctious child seated next to me. Time alone is a rare and precious commodity for busy moms. I look forward to flying simply for the peace and quiet, and opportunity to think without interruption.

But really! She didn't have to be so nasty!

I took the middle seat and placed Nathan in the aisle seat for her sake, thinking I could run interference if necessary. I didn't speak to her, and she didn't speak to me—until the meal arrived. Feeling awkward, I decided to break the tension with a typical question.

"So, what takes you to Nashville?" I asked.

"Business," came the cool reply, the woman's eyes fixed on her dinner tray.

I'm not sure why I took it any further. I could tell she really wasn't interested in conversing.

"What kind of business are you in?"

She went on to talk about some professional conferences she was attending and the workload that awaited her at the end of the line. I began to sense the immense pressures that had propelled the expletives out of her mouth. This poor woman was burned out.

We made small talk. I tried to keep the chitchat light and unintrusive. But what happened next surprised both of us.

"Mama! Mama!" Nathan exclaimed with glee.

"Yes, Nathan. What is it?" I responded, after excusing myself from the conversation.

At that moment, Nathan tapped his hands on his shoulders and flapped his hands out to the side.

"Nathan," I said with surprise, "do you see an angel?"

He gave an affirmative nod.

"Where do you see an angel?"

He pointed out the window to the wing of the airplane. Our seats were right over the wing.

The lady next to me leaned forward and said, "What's he trying to say?" She could tell he was adamant about getting through to me.

I wasn't sure what to expect, but I said, "Nathan says he sees an angel on the wing of the plane."

"Out there?" she exclaimed, pointing out the window.

I nodded. "Yes, right there."

After a long gaze out the window, she turned and looked at Nathan with tears in her eyes and said, "God knew I needed that."

Her response caught me completely off guard. Tears filled my eyes. Since all I had was Wet Wipes, the woman dug in her purse and gave me some tissues.

Amazing! I thought. *An hour ago, there was a wall of ice between us. Now we're sitting here blubbering together like two best friends.*

Only the Spirit of God can do that.

Once again I was overwhelmed by the extravagant love of God. He knew there was a woman on that plane who was exhausted and in need of encouragement. He cared enough to plant Nathan near her, and through a five-year-old mentally retarded boy, He delivered a blessing from beyond.

That incident was a gentle reminder to me that God is aware when we are feeling burned out. He is intimately acquainted with the burdens we carry and the pressures of the day. And He looks beyond our ugly attitudes and irreverent thoughts, seeing the deeper needs in our soul.

Oh, how much I want to be more like Him as I parent my children—to sense what is going on inside their hearts and be a hugger rather than a hammer.

To offer a smile rather than a scowl.

To say, "I believe in you" when they find it hard to believe in themselves.

To see the pain driving the profanity.

To listen rather than lecture.

To model rather than mandate.

To bring peace rather than pressure.

I don't know about you, but this kind of parenting often seems like an impossible assignment to me. Thank goodness we don't have to attempt it on our own. Only the Spirit of God can melt the walls of ice that chill our relationships. Only He can enable us to love extravagantly, like He does. Today, Lord, let it be.

The next time you notice a plane flying overhead, pause for a closer look. There could be an angel on the wing. From our experience, angels have a way of showing up when you don't have it all together, when your best foot isn't forward. The results are usually quite amazing.

Power Perk: A Taste of Hope

Separated from God, the soul dies. The consequence of living life independent from God is not a bad mood, nor a post-caffeine downer. It's a dead spirit.

—☕—

"Come, all you who are thirsty, come to the waters; and you who have no money, come, buy and eat!...Why spend money on what is not bread, and your labor on what does not satisfy? Listen, listen to me, and eat what is good, and your soul will delight in the richest of fare. Give ear and come to me; hear me, that your soul may live."

—Isaiah 55:1–3

—☕—

"Raising children is not unlike a long-distance race in which the contestants must learn to pace themselves....That is the secret of winning."

—James Dobson[1]

—☕—

"Call the Comforter by the term you think best—Advocate, Helper, Paraclete, the word conveys the indefinable blessedness of his sympathy; an inward invisible kingdom that causes the saint to sing through every night of sorrow. This Holy Comforter represents the ineffable motherhood of God."

—Oswald Chambers[2]

CHAPTER 3

The Hospital Chaplain

od is keeping careful watch over us and the future. The Day is coming when you'll have it all—life healed and whole...even though you have to put up with every kind of aggravation in the meantime."

—1 Peter 1:5–6, *The Message*

Our household had endured several months filled with aggravation. Little Ben, then three years old, had suffered through seven recurring ear infections, which meant many sleepless nights for him and me. Without sleep, I'm no good. Little things bug me, and I end up feeling like the Wicked Witch of the West.

With my pointed hat cocked, Benjamin and I headed for the hospital at 5:00 A.M. for his surgery. Everyone was hoping that tubes in his ears would be the solution. Dr. Delorit, in his green scrubs, greeted us with a smile, and the hospital staff took Ben to prep him for the procedure.

I sat in the waiting area sipping my latté while flipping through several magazines that didn't interest me. I don't like hospitals. And I didn't like the idea of Ben having general anesthetic. I'd heard plenty of tragic stories in my counseling office to fuel my worries. Trying my best not to let my imagination run wild, I prayed for the medical team, then tried to focus my attention on a magazine photo spread of prize-winning desserts. You know you're pooped out when a full-color glossy of a ten-layer chocolate decadence cake doesn't make you salivate.

An hour later, a nurse asked me to follow her as she carried my groggy little guy down the hall to a private room and handed him to me to rock until the anesthetic wore off. Ben nestled his head on my shoulder, and I soothed him and sang his favorite songs while he emerged from his slumber.

An older gentleman sauntered into our room, interrupting my creaky rendition of "Jesus Loves Me."

"How ya doing, honey?" he asked.

"Oh, I'm fine," I responded, noticing a peaceful presence about this grandfatherly man.

"And your little one?" he inquired.

"Oh, he's fine, too. Just a little groggy."

"Well, that's good," he said with a smile. "I'm the hospital chaplain, and I'm just checking on you. I like to watch out for those who come here."

I returned a smile and told him how nice it was that he took the time to care for people.

"It's what matters," he said with conviction. "Well, I'll be going now. I've got to check on the woman in the room across the way."

He shuffled slowly back to the door, but before disappearing, he turned and said, "You're a good mom."

Without warning, tears filled my eyes. For some reason, I really needed to hear those words. I didn't fully understand the surge of emotion that swelled within me. Perhaps it was due to the fatigue of months of interrupted sleep or the early morning reveille. Or maybe

I was just relieved that Ben was out of surgery and doing well.

But more likely, this kind man had placed a gentle, comforting hand on my hidden feelings of inadequacy—the feelings that surface when I face new situations and I'm not sure how to navigate…the feelings that come when standard behavioral techniques and parenting strategies seem to backfire…the feelings that are evoked when I realize I have less control over what happens to my kids than I prefer…the same feelings most conscientious moms and dads have now and then because they so desperately want to be good parents.

I leaned back in the rocker, sang a few more choruses, and hugged Ben tightly to me.

"You know what, little guy?" I whispered. "Everything is going to be all right. Before you know it, we'll be home again."

Ben and I went to the hospital that day because his ears needed some attention. God knew my ears needed something, too. So He sent a gracious chaplain my way to tell me: "You're a good mom."

My guess is you could use some words of comfort, too. You're sitting in the presence of a loving heavenly Father who has a message for you. Hear the whispers of His Spirit:

"I'm watching out for you."
"You're doing a good job."
"Everything is going to be all right."
"It won't be long before you're home."

Power Perk: A Sip of Humor

A grandmother was surprised by her seven-year-old grandson one morning. He had made her coffee! She drank what was the worst-tasting cup of coffee in her life. When she got to the bottom, there were three little green army men in her cup.

Puzzled, she asked, "Honey, what are the army men doing in my coffee?"

Her grandson answered, "Grandma, it says on TV, 'The best part of waking up is soldiers in your cup."

⸻

One summer evening during a violent thunderstorm, a mother was tucking her small boy into bed. She was about to turn off the light when he asked with a tremor in his voice, "Mommy, will you sleep with me tonight?"

The mother smiled and gave him a reassuring hug. "I can't, dear," she said. "I have to sleep in daddy's room."

A long silence was broken at last by his shaking little voice: "The big sissy."

CHAPTER 4

War Zones

A gentle answer turns away wrath."

—Proverbs 15:1

My heart went out to her. As a single mom with three adolescent girls, Teresa was trying her best to hold things together. It didn't take much discernment to see that she was clinically depressed. All the signs were there. Disrupted sleep. At three or four in the morning, she would lie fitfully awake, staring at the ceiling, unable to turn off the lights in her brain. Her concentration was scattered. Her fuse was short. Motivation was low, and an overwhelming heaviness weighed on her throughout the day.

"I really don't want to be here," she told me during our first session. "I've seen other counselors, and it didn't help. I'm only here because my pastor told me to come, and he's paying the bill."

I could tell we were off to a booming start.

"I appreciate your honesty, Teresa," I responded. "For some reason, you decided to come today. How would you like to use the hour so this isn't a complete waste of your morning?"

Her guard was up, but she went on to tell me that her kids were driving her crazy.

"They bicker. They fight," Teresa said glumly. "They act like they hate each other. They yell. They scream. They call me names and say they hate me. Anytime I say no to them, they blow a gasket and blast me with verbiage I wouldn't even want to repeat in front of you."

It was a common scenario. Unfair odds. Three kids to one punching bag (aka, Mom). This poor woman suffered a severe case of battle fatigue and honestly didn't know if she could survive one more day in the war zone. She had fantasized different ways of escape and concluded it would be best for everyone if she weren't "in the picture" anymore. She was convinced her children would be better off without her.

I knew there had to be more to the story. Dealing with obnoxious kids is a real pain, but it usually doesn't make a mom want to give up on life. A simple question uncovered the deeper issue.

"What usually happens inside you when you hear your kids fight?" I asked.

The dam broke and a flood of emotion came spilling out. For the next several minutes, I caught a glimpse of the anger and guilt that was driving Teresa's depression.

Four years earlier, her husband had left her for a younger woman. Now Teresa was thirty-nine and hurtling toward forty—a milestone she dreaded. Her girls were fifteen, thirteen, and eleven, and they were angry and confused. Legitimately so. Their father had abandoned them. But their mother was the one being shredded by their shrapnel. It wasn't fair that she was their emotional dumping ground, but it made sense. She was the only one the girls knew who would never turn on them. She was their safe place. That notion hadn't crossed Teresa's mind. All she knew was that she felt downright miserable and wanted to resign from life.

We talked briefly about the grief they all were suffering, and then we spent the rest of our time problem-solving. Teresa needed some practical tools to take home with her that day.

"Teresa, how do your girls behave at school?" I asked. "Do they comply with their teachers? Do they treat others respectfully?"

"Oh yes," she replied. "I get good reports. They aren't brilliant scholars, but their teachers tell me they enjoy having them in class."

"So you're telling me that your girls can contain their anger with their teachers and other classmates. Is that right?"

"Yes."

"Then that means they are quite capable of making better choices at home. If they can monitor their responses at school, they can learn to do it at home."

"I find it hard to believe you," she retorted. "You have no idea how bad it is. I don't think I'll ever be able to stop them from yelling at me. Particularly Cari."

She explained that Cari was the oldest daughter who set the example for the others to follow.

"You make a good point," I said. "You cannot control what comes out of their mouths. They are the only ones who can choose to control their words. But you do have the power to shape your girls with your responses and to let them know what you will or will not tolerate. Are you open to trying something different this week?"

She was ambivalent but agreed to brainstorm a plan.

A strategy evolved. Teresa decided the next time Cari blew up at her, she would not yell at her for being rude and disrespectful. She would address Cari in a quiet but firm voice and say, "Cari, I have feelings just like you. When you scream at me like that, it hurts me. I am not your enemy. I am on your side." Then she would refuse to engage in any further discussion until Cari cooled down.

Second-guessing the plan, Teresa said, "But I know exactly how Cari will respond. She'll say, 'There you go again, expecting me to be perfect.'

It's her favorite line whenever I ask her to make even a slight improvement."

I grinned and shook my head, realizing this strong-willed teenager knew how to slam dunk an argument.

"Teresa," I continued, "you don't have to let Cari bulldoze you like that. You can look her straight in the eye and say, 'Honey, I don't expect perfection, but I do expect common courtesy.'"

We went on to talk about the tremendous guilt Teresa carried because of the imperfections she saw in her daughters. She really believed their bad attitudes and conflicts were all her fault. She thought if she were a better mom, these things wouldn't be happening.

I tried to dismantle her false guilt with some simple stories. I told her about some teens I knew who would never think of saying a cross word to their parents. But it wasn't because their parents were wonderfully attentive and highly skilled in relationships. Their parents were raging addicts. The children complied out of fear. They were in survival mode. They didn't have the inner strength to challenge their parents. Frankly, the kids would have been healthier had they voiced their opinions now and then.

I also mentioned that I knew parents who were solid in their faith, heavily invested in being good parents, and yet their children made choices that created terrible pain for the entire family. Even God, who is a perfect father, has children who make choices against His will.

There are times when the equations of life don't make sense. The numbers don't add up. Not everything can be reduced to simple cause-and-effect.

"Some kids glide into this world more laid-back and compliant by nature," I told her. "Others burst into the delivery room in a flapping fit, ready to take on the world. Our children are not appendages of us. They're individuals in their own right, with a free will and genetically determined temperaments. Strong-willed kids happen to be harder nuts to crack, and it takes the pressures of difficult life circumstances to bring new definitions to their character."

She mulled this over for a few seconds and then glanced at the pictures on my desk. She saw my husband and three kids, all spit-shined and smiling—you know, the "perfect family" shot. Somehow I knew what was running through her mind, and out it came:

"Do your kids ever raise their voice at you?" she asked.

"Why, never! We all get along splendidly!" Then I laughed. "Of course they raise their voices at me. And, yes, I raise my voice at them, too. Sometimes I don't respond the way I really want to. But I'm working on it, and I hope to keep improving. Life is often a journey of three steps forward, two steps back."

As it turned out, Teresa came back to see me. And she kept coming. With the help of medication and regular exercise, her sleep was restored and her energy and mood began to level out. Gradually, she gained new courage to make changes at home. With the depression improved, Teresa more effectively offered her girls choices and consequences. She had the strength to clearly define household responsibilities and expectations. The changes she made influenced the entire family. The taller she stood, the more likely the girls were to follow in step. It was still three against one in their household, but Teresa eventually began to see that God and a single mom are a majority.

A turning point came one evening when Cari tried to engage Teresa in an all-out war. Teresa listened attentively, and when Cari paused to reload her ammo, Teresa squared her shoulders and said quietly, "Cari, I love you. And it hurts me when you yell at me like that." Then she turned on her heels, went to her bedroom, and locked the door.

A half hour later, Teresa heard a tentative knock at the door. Much to her astonishment, there stood Cari with puffy, red eyes.

"I'm sorry, Mom," she said through her tears.

That was several years ago. Teresa and I spent many hours together, processing the pain of their losses and strategizing about the challenges that come with parenting. Today, two of Teresa's daughters are in college and her youngest just graduated from high school. Their strong wills have propelled them forward in academic achievements and extracurricular activities. They are leaders among their peers.

Teresa's worst fear, that her daughters would desert her, never came to pass. I believe one of the keys to their progress was Teresa's choice to hold an ice cream social—otherwise known as a family meeting—with the girls each Sunday night. It was a time when Teresa mostly listened. Over ice cream, the girls talked about how the week went. They shared their joys and frustrations, helped each other solve problems, and prayed together.

The more the girls talked, the less they raged.

Emotional needs were met. The meetings lasted anywhere from ten minutes to a half hour. Not a huge chunk of time in a crowded schedule. Oh, they all still had their differences and bickered now and then. But for the most part, the battle cries were muted.

I ran into Teresa at the post office recently. She flagged me down and showed me a handmade card from Cari, who was away at college, that arrived just in time for Mother's Day. In big bold letters, the card said, "Mom, you're the best!" Inside was a letter thanking her for the many sacrifices she had made as a mom through the years.

Five years ago, Teresa couldn't imagine hearing anything positive from Cari.

It just goes to show you that the power of God can be released through a single mom who stands tall while dishing out gentle words—and ice cream sundaes.

Power Perk: A Taste of Hope

"Jesus stood and cried out, saying, 'If any man is thirsty, let him come to Me and drink. He who believes in me, as the Scripture said, 'From his innermost being shall flow rivers of living water.' But this He spoke of the Spirit."

—John 7:37–39, NASB

"I have often, myself, sat in darkness, and cried aloud for the Holy Spirit to deliver me from the fantasies that gather round a parched soul like flies round a rotting carcass in the desert. Likewise, I have sat tongue-tied, crying out to be given utterance, and delivered from the apprehensions that afflict the earth-bound. And never, ultimately, in vain. Jesus' promise is valid; the Comforter needs only to be summoned. The need is the call, the call is the presence, and the presence is the Comforter, the Spirit of Truth."

—Malcolm Muggeridge[1]

"Listen to me my chosen ones: The Lord who made you, who will help you says, O servant of mine, don't be afraid...For I will give you abundant water for your thirst and for your parched fields. And I will pour out my Spirit and my blessings on your children. They shall thrive."

—Isaiah 44:1–4, TLB

CHAPTER 5

Ruts

et us then approach the throne of grace with confidence, so that we may receive mercy and find grace to help us in our time of need."
—Hebrews 4:16

It was one of those days. Monday morning rolled around; I got the kids off to school, and all I wanted to do was go back to bed. I wasn't disheartened or troubled about anything in particular. I was just spent. My energy had been sucked dry by Little League, taxi driving, laundry, housekeeping, sibling rivalry, and too much output over the weekend. Everything in me was screaming, "No, no, no!" to all the go, go, go.

As I grabbed my cup of coffee from the kitchen counter, I noticed the "other" counter. You know, the counter—the one where everyone's important stuff gets plunked for safekeeping.

"I just cleaned that counter three days ago," I whined.

No one had bothered to comply with my sign: "Warning! This is not a garbage dump! Violators will be PROSECUTED!" Little wonder. Ben and Nathan didn't have the foggiest idea what the *P* word meant.

On a good day, I'd simply roll up my sleeves, dig into those prolific piles, and have the job conquered in an hour. Well, I'd at least have papers categorized and pushed into neat stacks so things looked more orderly.

This, however, was not a typical let's-jump-in-and-get-it-done kind of a day. I was in a rut with little motivation to climb my way out.

I doubt that many parents haven't felt this way at one time or another. Life has a way of digging deep trenches in our path and bulldozing us to the bottom of the hole. One day we're kicking up our heels, dancing down the road, enjoying the scenery. The next day we find ourselves sprawled out on our backsides with mud walls closing in on us. We're stuck in a rut. A slump. A funk. Whatever term you want to use, it's miserable.

Days come when we feel sluggish, out of sync, unfocused, and scattered. Sometimes it's hard to make sense of our experience. Life seems confusing. We don't feel good. Our emotions get jumbled. The pressures of parenting have a way of shaking up the categories of even the most secure.

There are days when we're overly sensitive. Our children look at us wrong, and we want to burst into tears. Our spouse makes a benign comment, and we read into it all kinds of hidden messages. Molehills become mountains. Laundry piles look like Mt. Everest. Fleeting thoughts become obsessions.

One dad told me, "I know I'm in a rut when I don't have the oomph to move the wet diaper from the changing table to the diaper pail."

Been there, done that.

What do you do when you're in a rut? Do you look frantically to other people to help you feel better? Do you search for a quick fix of approval? Do you fill your twenty-four-hour day with thirty-two hours of activity? Do you take things personally and work yourself into a tizzy? Do you withdraw and dig a trench in the gallon of mint chocolate chip ice cream? Do you turn yourself into a punching bag because you're not feeling 100 percent, thinking you should be at your best all the time?

The truth is, ruts are just another part of the journey. They are neither good nor bad in and of themselves. They are simply part of living in a physical body that has limitations. They're a natural by-product of having bodies that get tired, feelings that get hurt, and spirits that get demoralized.

Some days we feel more tired than others. And that's okay. We may not want to get out of bed until noon. (Although that's not an option for those of us with youngsters!) We're running on fumes instead of a full tank. From what I hear behind closed doors in the counseling office, this is a common theme among busy parents tending to 101 needs in a given day.

When we are in a rut, we don't have to multiply our misery by burying ourselves under a two-ton load of guilt. We don't have to be ashamed or disappointed that everything on the to-do list didn't get done. There are days when we simply cannot do all we would like to do. Our performance may even be sub-par. To keep pushing ourselves is about as effective as pressing harder on the remote control when the batteries are going dead. It gets us nowhere.

Oftentimes we'll find ourselves in a rut following periods of overexertion and extra output. Sometimes a slump is simply the body's way of shifting down to conserve energy, regroup, and restore. Our bodies are the first to tell us when we need to slow down.

The best prescription for the Slump Syndrome is grace. We give ourselves grace when we refuse to expect more from ourselves than we can possibly deliver. We give ourselves grace when we grant ourselves permission to rest, sleep, play, take a break, and get alone with

God. A few minutes of quiet interaction with God can get us out of a rut much faster than striving, trying harder, and forcing ourselves into overdrive.

There are lessons to be learned in ruts. We won't always understand the full meaning of the lessons until we're further down the path. But for now we need to trust that God is up to something good, even in the ruts. Even when things don't happen the way we want. Even when little makes sense, and we feel buried under life's demands.

Next time you're in a rut, be gentle with yourself. Rest. Take a break. Quiet your mind. Clarity will more likely come when you are peaceful than when you are pushing so hard. Close the door on the clutter and open your heart in the throne room. Ask God to speak to you. Listen carefully.

On days when it feels as if the walls are caving in on you and your backside is caked in mud, remember that God can do amazing things with a little bit of mud. He created Adam from it. He healed the blind man with it. The woman caught in adultery found freedom as she read His inscriptions in it. I wonder what surprises He has in store for those of us who are pooped-out parents today. The rule of grace says that His blessings can be found even at the bottom of a rut.

Power Perk: A Sip of Humor

A family in the east was planning a month's vacation on the West Coast. At the last minute, the father's work responsibilities prevented him from going, but Mom insisted that she was capable of driving and that she and the kids would go ahead. Dad got out the maps and planned the route and where the family should stop each night.

A couple of weeks later, the father completed his extra work responsibilities. He decided to surprise the family, so he flew to a West Coast city without calling them. Then he took a taxi out into the country on a highway that, according to his travel plan, the family should be driving on later that day. The taxi driver dropped him off on the side of the road. Dad waited there until he saw the family car coming, then stuck out his thumb like a hitchhiker. As Mom and the kids drove past, they did a double take. One of the kids said, "Hey, wasn't that Dad?" Mom screeched to a stop, backed up to the hitchhiker, and the family had a joyful reunion.

Later, when a newspaper reporter asked the man why he would do such a crazy thing, he responded, "After I die, I want my kids to be able to say, 'Dad sure was fun, wasn't he?'"[1]

Chapter 6

Best Friends

*T*herefore I tell you, whatever you ask for in prayer, believe that you have received it, and it will be yours."

—Mark 11:24

It was scary for a little boy to leave behind all his buddies and move to an unfamiliar neighborhood in Chicago. Oh, the new house was fine, and the yard was peppered with gigantic maple trees to climb, but it wasn't the same. Darrell missed his other home.

But one day he mustered the courage to peek over the high wooden fence into his new neighbor's yard. His little knuckles turned white as he gripped the fence boards to climb his way to the top. The few splinters that buried themselves in his soft skin didn't hurt after his eyes glimpsed something he hadn't expected—another little boy, about the same size and age, playing alone on a swing set.

"Hi!" Darrell called to his neighbor.

"Hi!" came the response. "What's your name?"

"Darrell. What's yours?"

"Scotty."

"Oh," Darrell replied, not sure what to say next.

"You want to swing?" asked Scotty.

"Sure!" Darrell smiled and scaled the fence.

From that moment on, the two boys were inseparable. Lying side by side, bellies on the carpet, feet in the air, and chins cupped in their hands, they began their days watching *Captain Kangaroo* and *Mr. Green Jeans*. It didn't matter that they couldn't tell whether or not his jeans were really green on the black-and-white TV.

Darrell loved summer best. The boys whiled away the afternoon hours building castles in the sandbox, playing cowboys and Indians, and climbing the wonderful maples that towered high above them in the backyard. In the heat of the day, they ran through the sprinklers as long as their moms allowed. Just about the time the neatly manicured grass reached its saturation point and looked more like a muddy swamp than a Chem-lawn, the Good Humor Man jingled his way around the corner. Racing as fast as their little legs could carry them, Darrell and Scotty chased after the truck with their fists clenched full of nickels. Nothing could top those lip-smacking Fudgesicles!

Every now and then Darrell's dad came home from work and waved the boys over saying, "How would you like to go out for a hamburger?" In five seconds flat, they piled into Dad's new shiny red-and-white Ford Edsel station wagon and did some male bonding over twelve-cent burgers and twenty-five-cent milk shakes.

But there was one day each week that Darrell and Scotty parted company—Sunday. When Darrell dressed up in his best clothes, Scotty roamed in his pajamas. Darrell begged his pal to come to church with him, but Scotty's family always had other things to do. It just never worked out.

One hot summer day Darrell's father announced that he had taken a new job and the family would be moving to a different home. At first, Darrell was excited about the new adventure, but he quickly realized he'd be leaving Scotty behind. That night, Darrell cried himself to sleep. He couldn't imagine not being able to play with Scotty.

Eventually, the day of the big move arrived. After the last box was loaded into the station wagon, Darrell and Scotty hugged a time or two and said their final sad good-byes. Darrell's mom brushed away the tears as she watched her little boy experience his first major loss.

Several days later, Darrell's mom noticed the gloom in her son's eyes. She knew life would be full of losses and disappointments for her young man and wanted to help him learn an important lesson. Setting Darrell on her lap, she said, "Honey, even though we don't live next door to Scotty anymore, and we can't see him every day, there is something we can do for him?"

A glimmer of hope appeared on Darrell's face, and he asked, "Like what?"

"We can pray for him."

Darrell didn't think that sounded nearly as exciting as playing in the sprinklers or sharing a Fudgesicle, but he decided to go along with the idea. Every morning he prayed for Scotty before breakfast. Then he prayed again when *Captain Kangaroo* and *Mr. Green Jeans* came on TV. His dinnertime blessing became a ritual: "Thank you, God, for this food and bless Scotty." And every night when he finished his bedtime prayers, Darrell asked God for one more thing, "And please, God, bless Scotty."

* * * *

Darrell began school, and as the years went by, he finished junior high, high school, college, and graduate school. He married and started a family of his own. Every so often, when he heard the bells of an ice cream truck or watched his own children playing in the sprinklers, he thought of Scotty and remembered the boy who was his first best friend.

A while back, Darrell, his wife, and four children took a vacation and paid a visit to his old house with the giant maple trees. The fence was gone, but the trees had more than doubled in size. Darrell told his children all about his fun-filled days with Scotty, the boy next door. And when the kids had had enough reminiscing, they all piled into their shiny red minivan and did some family bonding at the local McDonald's over 70¢ burgers and $1.50 milk shakes.

In keeping with the Dahlman clan tradition, the next morning the family decided to visit Willow Creek Community Church with their extended clan. The old hymns evoked a flood of memories of days gone by. But nothing moved Darrell more than what happened in the church foyer after the service. As they were leaving, his mother turned to him and said, "Darrell, I'd like you to meet a family who has just started coming to church."

Darrell turned to greet a balding, middle-aged man, his wife and two children.

As he carefully studied the eyes of this man, his mother asked, "Do you remember?"

At once he knew.

"You're Scotty!" Darrell exclaimed. "My first best friend!"

After thirty-seven years, they hugged a time or two and marveled that their paths had crossed once again.

To an older, more cynical observer, a little boy's prayers might seem trivial and meaningless. A waste of time. Wishful thinking. Sentimental mumbo jumbo. But Darrell's mom saw things from another perspective. She was convinced her little boy's two-word prayers such as "Bless Scotty" made a difference. Simple prayers were significant. She taught her son to use his pain as a springboard for prayer.

It just goes to show that sophisticated eloquence and rhetoric don't matter much. But a simple prayer of faith can change a life, even after thirty-seven years. That truth applies to little boys who watch *Captain Kangaroo* as well as grown-up men and women who watch their grandkids waving their green dollar bills while chasing down an ice cream truck.

Power Perk: A Taste of Hope

"Human problems are never greater than divine solutions."

—Irwin W. Lutzer[1]

"Don't bargain with God. Be direct. Ask for what you need. This is not a cat-and-mouse, hide-and-seek game we're in."

—Luke 11:10, *The Message*

"Pray not for lighter burdens but for stronger backs."

—Theodore Roosevelt[2]

"Don't fret or worry. Instead of worrying, pray. Let petitions and praises shape your worries into prayers, letting God know your concerns. Before you know it, a sense of God's wholeness, everything coming together for good, will come and settle you down. It's wonderful what happens when Christ displaces worry at the center of your life."

—Philippians 4: 6–7, *The Message*

CHAPTER 7

God Cares about What Matters to Us

I s any one of you in trouble? He should pray."

—James 5:13

John and I have known Jill and Theo for years. Their twin boys, Jeff and Ted, were part of the first junior high youth group John pastored many moons ago. We've watched these handsome young men and their younger brother, Eric, grow into adulthood, get married, and start families of their own. I was talking with Jill a while back, and she told me a story from their family journal that likely will be passed on to their future generations. It's the kind of reminder that pooped-out parents need, and you might enjoy reading it to your kids, too. I'll let Jill tell the story in her own words....

* * * *

Because Jeff and Ted are identical twin sons, we got them identical yellow Schwinn Stingray bicycles when they were ten years old. Like most energetic, all-American boys their age, they spent nearly every waking moment riding through the neighborhoods on adventurous escapades. Their routine was like clockwork. After school, they did homework, then zoomed off on their bicycles until it was time for dinner.

One evening, they gobbled down their meals, asked permission to be excused, and bolted out the door. Seconds later, we heard a frantic cry.

"Hey! Where's my bike? Oh no! Somebody stole my bike!"

Theo and I ran outside and discovered we had been robbed.

We couldn't believe it. While our family was sitting around the dinner table on the other side of the door, someone had walked into our garage and swiped Jeff's bike.

"Why my bike?" lamented Jeff.

Ted piped in, "Oh, so you wish they had taken mine!"

"Sure! No, not really. I just can't believe it's gone."

The boys were devastated, and Theo and I were furious. After all, the bike wasn't cheap.

We all were standing in the garage, feeling stunned and disappointed, when Theo said, "Wait a minute. Boys, do you remember what we were talking about the other day? Remember how we decided we were going to pray when things go wrong? Well, that's what we need to do right now."

Jeff sighed. "Guess it couldn't hurt."

We all joined hands in the garage, and Theo prayed that the person who took the bike would be overwhelmed with guilt for stealing it.

"Yeah, God, make him feel really guilty," Jeff added fervently.

Theo went on to pray that the thief would abandon the bike, and it would be returned to us. A hearty "Amen!" was said by all.

One day went by without any word. Then two. Then a week. Ted tried to buffer the blow by letting Jeff take turns on his bike. But even so, it was hard on Jeff. I felt sad watching my little boy left behind while his brother and friends zipped down the driveway and out of sight. A few nights later, I told Theo we needed to think seriously about buying a new bike.

"Let's wait a few more days," he said with assurance. "I really think the bike is going to show up."

I wanted to believe the best, but after waiting seven days, I was discouraged.

The next day as I was tidying the house, the phone rang. A woman on the other end of the line said, "Are you missing a yellow bike?"

"Yes!" I shrieked. "It was stolen out of our garage!"

"Well, I think I found it," she continued. "This morning when I went out to get my newspaper, my dog bolted out the door and ran across the street and into the woods. She's an indoor dog, and I was afraid she'd get lost, so I went after her. I ran toward the woods, calling her name again and again. When I stopped to catch my breath, I heard her barking and followed the sound. There she was, yipping frantically at a yellow bicycle like it was another dog trespassing on her turf. I figured the bike had been abandoned since there wasn't another person in sight. I headed home thinking someone would come back for the bike, but something inside told me to go back and wheel it home with me."

Hardly pausing to take a breath, the woman continued.

"After a closer look, I noticed there was a store sticker on the chrome with an identification number. I felt compelled to call the store. They checked their records and gave me your name and phone number. Evidently you've moved since you purchased the bike because the number they gave me was disconnected. I called directory assistance, and they gave me this number. Anyway, that's a long story just to say I have your bike, and if you'd like to come pick it up, I'll give you directions."

I penciled out a map to her home and relayed the good news to Theo, Jeff, and Ted. The boys jumped up and down like a couple of wild kangaroos and begged to leave *that* minute.

Before we piled into the car, Theo said, "Jeff, do you remember the prayer we said together after your bike was stolen?"

Jeff's eyes widened as big as silver dollars, and with seven days of stored-up ten-year-old energy, he blurted out, "God really knew how much I wanted my bike back, didn't He, Dad!"

Choking back the tears, Theo said, "Yes, Jeff. God cares about the things that matter to us."

We found our Good Samaritan's house a few miles away, with Jeff's bike waiting safely outside. It was dirty but still in good condition. The gratitude written all over Jeff's face was the only repayment the woman needed. Theo and I expressed our appreciation to this complete stranger for going to great lengths to return the bike.

I'm not sure what our "doggedly determined" friend thought that day when we stopped by her home. I've often wondered if she realized she was heaven's helper in answering a desperate boy's prayers, spoken seven days earlier in a cold, dark garage.

* * * *

Today, Jeff and Ted are each married with several children of their own. They, too, have moments of feeling pooped out, discouraged, and worn thin by the challenges of parenting active little ones. But their mom and dad taught them well. When things go wrong, they take a few minutes to stop, join hands with their loved ones, and ask for God's help. Of the many childhood memories they have filed away, the yellow bike story is a fresh reminder of God's careful attention to every detail of their lives. And you can bet that some evening around the dinner table, their kids will hear that God cares about what matters to them, too.

But I have a sneaking suspicion the garage door will be shut tight and triple bolted.

Power Perk: A Sip of Humor

A minister walked by a group of teenagers who were sitting on the church lawn and stopped to ask what they were doing.

"Oh, nothing much, Pastor," replied one lad. "We're just seeing who has told the biggest fib about his sex life."

"Boys! Boys! Boys!" intoned the minister. "I'm shocked. When I was your age, I never even thought about kissing a girl."

The boys looked at each other, and then all replied in unison, "You win, Pastor!"

"If there is a fountain of youth, it is almost certainly caffeinated!"
—Sherri Weaver[1]

CHAPTER 8

Percolating Prayers

*A*nd *pray in the Spirit on all occasions...."*

—Ephesians 6:18

I have friends who spend hours each day interceding in prayer. Their children are grown and gone, and they can devote extended time to supplication. I'm not in the same phase of life. Sure, I pray daily, and I have a prayer journal I write in consistently. But during these busy years when my three children consume most of my waking hours, I also find strength in little prayers. I like to call them "percolating prayers."

All kinds of these short, power-packed prayers pop up throughout the Gospels:

> The disciples prayed, "Lord, save us!"
> The troubled mother prayed, "Lord, help me!"
> The soldier cried, "Lord, my servant is suffering...."
> The teacher of the Law said, "Teacher, I will follow you...."
> The leper said, "Lord, you can make me clean...."
> The blind man called out, "Have mercy on us, Lord...."

Today, my little prayers went something like this:

> "Surround us with your love."

"Teach me."

"Fill us with your Spirit."

"Help me to be patient."

"Please give the kids wisdom."

"The kids need your guidance."

"Thank you, Lord."

"Wow, God! You are awesome!"

Some prayers are requests for help. Others simply acknowledge the facts. The form or shape of the prayer really doesn't matter. There are no restrictions on when or where these prayers can percolate. Send them heavenward while you're throwing dolls and Matchbox cars in the toy box for the umpteenth time, or while you're standing in line at the grocery store, or when you're stuck in rush-hour traffic.

For those of us who are pooped-out parents, what matters most is that we connect with God and link our soul with our Source. As the gentle touch of a light switch generates power to illuminate a room, so, too, our little prayers connect us with God and release His energy to empower us for the day.

Power Perk: A Taste of Hope

"God looks at the intention of the heart rather than the gifts He is offered."

—John Pierre Camus[1]

⸺⸺

"We plan the way we want to live, but only GOD makes us able to live it."

—Proverbs 16:9, *The Message*

⸺⸺

"The Spirit of God alters my dominating desires; he alters the things that matter, and a universe of desires I had never known before suddenly comes on the horizon."

—Oswald Chambers[2]

⸺⸺

"It takes wisdom to build a house, and understanding to set it on a firm foundation."

—Proverbs 24:3, *The Message*

⸺⸺

"Out of the mouth of babes comes things we should have said in the first place."

—Anonymous[3]

CHAPTER 9

A Cure for Frazzled Family Syndrome

And we pray that God, by His power, will fulfill all your good intentions and faithful deeds."

—2 Thessalonians 1:11, NLT

If you're anything like me, you can identify with the adage, "A parent's work is never done." We have too much to do, in too little time. Guilt and frustration pile up when we can't be in three places at once. It's a juggling act to balance family life. There are seasons in the year when the screenplay in our home should be titled *Little House on the Freeway* rather than *Little House on the Prairie.*

It's amazing how quickly schedules can change from one week to the next. Routines get chaotic overnight. Calendars fill up and choke out any free time.

Not long ago, our family had some back-to-back weeks from you know where. Ben started football with Dad coaching his team. Practices were held two nights a week, and games were played on Saturday. Jessie was already full swing into volleyball, attending practices and games three afternoons a week. As I was picking up Jessie after her activities, John and Ben were leaving for theirs. These comings and goings were added to lives already brimming with school, church, and work obligations. We considered installing a revolving door at the entrance to our house.

After a couple of weeks of this new rat race routine, I was whipped. It felt as if our family had been sucked into a tornado and sent spinning in every direction. I crawled into bed that night realizing we had not shared one dinner around the table for two weeks. It grieved me. Those weren't my intentions. How did this happen?

Dinner had always been the time to connect with each other after full days. John and I enjoyed hearing about the kids' school experiences and what was on their minds. Oh, there were occasions when we asked, "What happened at school today?" only to have the kids shrug and say, "Nothing." But usually we were able to glean bits and pieces from their world as we shoveled down the four basic food groups. It was one little portion of the day I counted on to help our family establish a sense of "us."

That Friday night, I pulled the covers up close and mentally walked through the week one more time. As I sorted through what had happened, a scene from the counseling office replayed itself. I was sitting across from a sixteen-year-old girl who was telling me what was "wrong" at home. In the middle of a long string of complaints, she said, "We never eat together as a family. Everyone just grabs something from the freezer, nukes it, and eats in front of the TV." Then she said something that surprised me, coming as it did from an independent, mildly rebellious teen. Looking at the floor, she shook her head and said, "It doesn't feel like we're a family."

As I lay awake looking at the ceiling, I could identify with her. I didn't feel like we were much of a family either by the end of that fourteen-day dash. I knew things needed to change. Somehow we had to find a way to regroup and conserve some positive energy for family connections.

I didn't remember life being this frantic when I was growing up. Dinners together were a given. Mom cooked. We ate. Sometimes dad wasn't home because of business trips, but even so, the rest of us gathered around the table.

Those memories left me with another dilemma. I faced the challenge of resolving the conflict between expectations stemming from my family history and the realities of my current daily life. As I saw it, I had two options: stay stuck and bury myself under a heaping pile of guilt or find a solution. Since I hate playing the guilt game, I chose to problem-solve.

We planned a barbecue for Sunday evening and a round-robin discussion on the issue. I wanted help from everyone—creative ideas, brainstorms, answers, anything to help us get back on track. I wanted to procure a collective commitment.

Well, we didn't completely cure our frazzled family syndrome in one night, but we did come up with some ideas. When we looked at the following week's work, school, and sports schedules, we discovered there were three nights we could sit down together to a meal if we ate later than usual. During dinner, the answering machine would go on duty. And Mom and Dad set aside their role as disciplinarians. Corrections had to wait. The dinner table was off-limits as an emotional dumping ground.

The kids decided they wanted to switch family night to Sundays. That's our evening to have an early dinner, play games, make popcorn, sit around the fire, watch a movie, or do whatever the group votes on. It's protected time to reconnect and strengthen family ties.

The old saying goes, "If you aim at nothing, you're sure to hit it."

That certainly applies to building a strong family. In our hectic and hurried culture, we have to fight for cohesion because so many enticements lure us away from one another. I believe this is one of Satan's subtle schemes to destroy our emotional and spiritual well-being.

The quality of family life stems from the individual daily choices we make. Most of us have far more power than we think to create positive change. If we feel stuck, we don't have to stay stuck. External forces endeavoring to pull us apart will always be present, but we don't have to allow them to rule our lives by default. We can be intentional and proactive. We can decide to make adjustments and improvements.

Don't get me wrong. Our family doesn't hit the bull's-eye every day of every week. But we're much more on target than we were during that frantic, frenzied stretch. Even when things don't work out as planned, I find peace knowing that we are actively working toward the goal of sane schedules and tight family bonds. And I'm comforted to know that God has every intention of helping our intentions come to pass. When our efforts falter, God is faithful. By His power and grace, He'll keep us moving in the right direction.

So how was your week? If the fabric of your family life is coming apart thread by thread, take action. Don't merely throw up your hands and say, "Everyone's busy and stressed out. That's just the way life is in our fast-paced society." Gather your troop together and make tough decisions. Clear your calendar. Abolish some activities. Regulate your routine. Revamp responsibilities. Overcome overload. Then reap the rewards of more time with the most important people in your life.

Power Perk: A Sip of Humor

* You know you're fatigued when you sit at a stop sign waiting for it to turn green.

* You know you're fatigued when you find yourself peering into the refrigerator wondering if you just put something away, or if you were needing to take something out.

* You know you're fatigued when you find yourself licking the bottom of your coffeepot.

* You know you're fatigued when you send your kids next door to borrow a cup of Prozac.

Out of the mouth of babes...

Dear Pastor,
I know God loves everybody, but He never met my sister.
Ben, age 7

Dear Pastor,
Please say a prayer for our flag football team. We need God's help or a quarterback.
Tommy, age 9

Dear Pastor,
My father says I should learn the Ten Commandments. But I don't think I want to because we have enough rules in my   house already.
Jeremy, age 6

Dear Pastor,
Are there any devils on earth? I think there may be one in my class.
Carla, age 10

CHAPTER 10

Birthday Blowouts

*[*G*od] does not ignore the prayers of men in trouble when they call to him for help."*

—Psalm 9:12, TLB

If you haven't read the story of his traumatic entry into this world in *Angel Behind the Rocking Chair*, then you need to know that Nathan's birth was a seismic jolt to our family. Our surprise package arrived six weeks early with life-threatening heart complications and Down Syndrome.

As a therapist, one of my specialty areas is working with individuals suffering from post-traumatic stress disorder. These people experienced an event that was catastrophic or posed a serious threat to them or a loved one. Some trauma victims have flashbacks and nightmares, and they frequently find it difficult to sleep at night and concentrate during the day.

During the years following Nathan's arrival, I found it hard to admit that *I* struggled with some of those symptoms. I suffered from spontaneous feelings of impending doom, irrational fears that a family member would be harmed or killed, and a heightened sense of anxiety I had never known before.

The fear of Nathan dying was legitimate for a while. But then things changed. God healed his heart, and Nathan's strength increased. The possibility of losing him was no longer a medical reality. But the issue remained for me because my fears never quite subsided.

I used all the therapeutic interventions I knew to combat the unwelcome anxiety. Healthy self-talk, diversions, debriefing with friends, exercise, prayer, Scripture reading, singing praise songs. You name it, I did it. And much of the time, I found relief.

But there was a day when…well, relief didn't come.

It was Ben's ninth birthday. Ten boys joined us at the local roller skating rink for chocolate cake, ice cream, presents, and a great time of blading to the beat. I had just skated off the rink after dancing the Hokey Pokey with Nathan when it happened…again. A surge of looming calamity swept over me, and I found myself wrestling with dark images of one of the kids getting hurt.

This is ridiculous, I said to myself. *I'm not giving in to this fear. This is my son's birthday!*

I prayed, "Lord, I thank you for all the children who came to Ben's party today. Please protect every one of them from harm and danger. Keep them safe and watch over our time together."

I then forced myself to focus on something else, and the fear dissolved.

About an hour later, Ben and his friend, whom we call "Little Ben," were skating around the rink with John. Little Ben said, "Hey, John, let me skate through your legs." So he crouched down and smoothly zipped under John.

I grabbed my camera and yelled, "Hey, you guys! Do that again so I can get a picture."

They came around a second time, and Little Ben took position, aimed, and again whizzed through in perfect style. The guys were grinning from ear to ear.

Next time around, it was our Ben's turn. He lined up, squatted down, headed under John's legs…and promptly initiated a jarring collision. Ben's skate caught John's, and they both went flying through the air. John landed on top of Ben, smacking his head into the floor. I quickly realized I was taking a picture of a major wipeout. The next thing I saw was Ben holding his bloody mouth and frantically wailing, "My teeth! My teeth! My teeth!"

With adrenaline coursing through my veins, I hopped the railing to help. Sure enough, through the bloody mess I could see that half of Ben's two front teeth were gone. John's eyes met mine and mirrored the panic and alarm I felt.

Trying to reassure Ben, John said, "It's going to be okay, Ben. The dentist can fix your teeth. You're a brave boy. Come on, let's get off the rink."

John took Ben to the rest room to get towels, and I grabbed my cell phone to call the dentist. We caught him just in time. Dr. Monnes was putting on his coat to leave for the day but told us to immediately bring Ben to the office. John stayed at the rink until the other boys' parents arrived. I drove Ben to the dentist's office and sat beside him as the doctor went to work on his teeth.

On the outside, I maintained composure for Ben's sake. But inside, I was a torrent of swirling emotions. I was sad that Ben's beautiful permanent teeth were ruined. I was angry that this mishap happened right after my fervent prayer for protection. On the way to the dentist's office, I wondered why I'd even bothered to pray. It felt like God had ignored my prayers. I wanted so much to be rid of the irrational fears that had plagued me since Nathan's birth. I had been making progress…and now this.

I sat by Ben, numbly watching the procedure, and asked the

doctor if the nerves would live. If the nerves were severely damaged, Ben would need two root canals and permanent caps put on. Dr. Monnes wasn't certain and said we would have to watch them over time. I'm not sure where the energy came from, but I interrupted the process and said, "I'd like to stop for a minute and pray for Ben—and for his teeth." The doctor and his assistant agreed and paused for a moment.

Laying my hand on Ben's chest, I said, "God, please touch the nerves in Ben's teeth and let them live. And give Ben Your peace. And please, Lord, bless Dr. Monnes in everything he does tonight to help Ben. Amen." Ben sat patiently while Dr. Monnes skillfully bonded composite material to his remaining stubs, forming two adultlike teeth.

Two hours later, Ben hopped out of the chair with two "new" front teeth and asked to go to Burger King. I marveled at his resiliency and secretly wished I could have accepted the mishap as easily as he did.

"God, what happened?" I asked over and over that night. It's a question many parents ask when prayers for their children seem to go unanswered.

The following day, I went for a walk with my friend Joy. I told her about Ben's birthday crisis and my bewilderment. Wise friend that she is, she said, "There are no pat answers in situations like this, but I believe God will give you a personal answer."

I told Joy how much I wanted to hear the Lord's perspective and then said, "I really shouldn't be bellyaching. This is nothing compared to what my cousin Jim and his wife, Suzanne, have gone through."

Their twelve-year-old son, Caleb, suffered from life-threatening heart complications. One day, Jim, a medical doctor, had returned from his daily run and was checking his pulse. Caleb asked to have his pulse checked, too. To Jim's horror, he discovered that Caleb's heart was beating so rapidly he couldn't keep count. His resting pulse was off the charts. Jim immediately called the hospital and ordered a battery of tests for the next day. The discovery was "incidental." The family had no prior awareness that Caleb had a heart condition. He was an accomplished gymnast and looked like the epitome of youthful, energetic health. After seven hours of testing, the doctors reported a diagnosis of ventricular tachacardia, a condition that can cause death. Various medications were tried to no avail.

When I finished telling Joy this story, she got a quizzical look on her face and said, "Aren't those the same cousins with the little boy whose teeth God healed?"

She was right. Somehow she remembered the story I told during one of our walks the previous summer— a story I'd forgotten until she mentioned it.

Jim and Suzanne's son Luke was born without one adult tooth bud. Routine X rays revealed this when Luke was seven years old. Suzanne and Caleb had the same condition. As the children approached the age when orthodontics might be necessary, Suzanne envisioned writing out check after check for treatment. A friend of hers challenged her to pray for her children's teeth rather than passively resign to the fact that all six of her kids would need braces. So Suzanne asked God to guide her children's teeth to the right place in their mouths.

Several years later, when Luke was eleven, he went to the dentist for his annual checkup and cleaning. New X rays were taken. But when the nurse gave the dentist the films, he reviewed them and said, "You've given me the wrong pictures. These aren't Luke's. They must be someone else's."

The nurse double-checked and assured the dentist that the X rays were Luke's. On closer examination, the dentist realized that he did have the correct film and that he was staring at something unexplainable. Leaving Luke in the chair, he went to the waiting room to show Suzanne the pictures.

"Look here!" he said. "The X rays we took before show an adult tooth bud missing. The X rays we took today show a tooth in that same space!"

"Wow!" Suzanne exclaimed. "Do you think this is a bona fide dental miracle?"

The dentist nodded his head and said he'd never seen anything like it.

With Luke's story fresh in my mind, I said to Joy, "Okay, let's think about this. I prayed for my son, and half of his front teeth got knocked out. Suzanne prayed for her son and—poof!—a tooth appears out of nowhere. So what do I make of that?"

With a smirk, Joy replied, "It's obvious. The only conclusion is that God plays favorites!"

We both laughed, knowing that neither of us believed that to be true. But my question was still hanging. We finished our walk and decided the dilemma was too complex for our brains to work with at the time.

In the days that followed, I asked God to speak to me. I needed encouragement and perspective. During quiet moments in front of the fire, I jotted some thoughts in my journal in the form of personal instructions from God to me:

• "Do not assume your prayers were not answered simply because things didn't turn out as you wanted. Things could have been far worse."

• "Surrender again to My sovereignty over your family. No matter what happens, I am with you."

- "I am more concerned with character than cosmetics. Benjamin displayed courage and patience. Celebrate his strong character."

- "You pray for strength. You yearn to be as resilient as your child. I saw this resiliency in you when you were wrestling with doubt and yet instinctively prayed for Ben's teeth in the dentist's office."

- "Let your anxiety be a reminder of your utter dependence on Me. Your faith is growing. Do not despise the growth pains. Endure with the strength that I give."

- "Your doubts do not intimidate Me. Keep praying, even when in doubt. Your feelings do not influence my response; your faith does."

- "You will never experience life as if the trauma surrounding Nathan's birth didn't happen. Acknowledge and embrace that scar. Give yourself permission to grieve when necessary. But do not despise your weakness or hope for the scar to disappear. When others saw My scars, their faith increased."

- "Accept your scars and trust they are etched in your soul for a purpose. Watch and see the redemptive value I will give them."

On the heels of trauma or during times of difficult transition, anxiety is often exaggerated. Our psychological defenses are weakened by severe or chronic stress, making it more difficult to ward off worries. The unpredictable nature of life seems magnified and keeps us from enjoying the positive aspects of our journey. When we are pooped out, fear screams, "Yesterday was bad, today is horrible, and tomorrow will be even worse." It can be difficult to believe the best. Ah, but these are also the times when our faith can take quantum leaps forward.

Many of the dilemmas life brings us don't have easy, tidy answers. But God will have personal answers for us if we risk asking tough questions and then take time to listen. Why not quiet your heart, open the Scriptures, and listen to what the Holy Spirit is saying to you in the midst of your circumstances? Surrender your fears about your children to the Lord.

Life is hard, but God is good. In spite of how things may appear, or how jumbled our emotions may feel, God is working in our lives and our children's lives when we surrender them to Him.

I caught a glimpse of this principle the other day when Ben proudly examined his new smile in the mirror and hummed, "All I want for Christmas are my two front teeth."

Postscript: Over a year has passed since Ben's accident, and the nerves in his teeth are still alive.

Power Perk: A Taste of Hope

"It's impossible to please God apart from faith. And why? Because anyone who wants to approach God must believe both that he exists and that he cares enough to respond to those who seek him."

—Hebrews 11:6, *The Message*

"If all things are possible with God, then all things are possible to him who believes in Him."

—Corrie Ten Boom, 1892–1982[1]

"To believe with certainty, we must begin with doubting."

—Stanislaw J. Lec, 1909–1966[2]

"[Jesus] said, 'I'm telling you, once and for all, that unless you return to square one and start over like children, you're not even going to get a look at the kingdom, let alone get in. Whoever becomes simple and elemental again, like this child, will rank high in God's kingdom.'"

—Matthew 18:2–3, *The Message*

CHAPTER 11

The Prayers of a Ten-Year-Old Availeth Much

"Now glory be to God, who by his mighty power at work within us is able to do far more than we would ever dare to ask or even dream of— infinitely beyond our highest prayers, desires, thoughts, or hopes."
—Ephesians 3:20, TLB

Ten-year-olds are terrific. They have reached a plateau where they are assimilating, balancing, and consolidating their resources. They haven't yet hit the roller-coaster mood swings and emotional upheavals attached to puberty. Therapists often refer to the tenth year as the golden age of transition because the wonderful aspects of childhood seem to peak at this time. It's a time when children are relatively even tempered, and they begin to think beyond themselves. They ask thoughtful questions and are genuinely interested in how things work. This curiosity often overlaps into spiritual areas as well. There's a burgeoning inquisitiveness about who God is, where He came from, and His relevance to this world.

My friend Lisa and I were visiting over lattés one afternoon when she told me about a life-changing event that happened when she was ten. She was a sensitive and reflective child who spent many summer evenings lying on the grass, gazing at the stars, and pondering the reality of God. They were deep thoughts for a little girl: Is God real? Does He exist like my parents say? Is it true that He knows every thought that goes through my mind? Does He really hear my prayers? Lisa wanted to believe what her parents told her about God, but she also wanted tangible proof.

Each afternoon, Lisa walked to the nearby post office with the family dog to mail letters for her parents. One day, she decided to test the reality of God. Skipping down the sidewalk with her schnauzer, Lisa prayed, "*God, if You really exist, please prove it to me. Please put a one-dollar bill on the sidewalk in front of me.*" She figured a kid could buy a lot of Bazooka bubble gum for a buck!

All the way to the post office, Lisa carefully searched for the divine dollar. She was certain God would position it strategically for her to discover. By the time she reached the mailbox, however, all her little eyes had seen were cracks, pebbles, and a bunch of rough cement.

Feeling dejected, Lisa headed home. Back to the home where Mom and Dad talked confidently about God. Back to the home where worship songs were heard each day. Back to the home where she watched her mother kneel in prayer over all the children. Back to the home where God seemed so close to others, but so far from her.

Lisa's eyes scouted every square centimeter of concrete between the post office and home. Her pockets remained empty. "No Bazooka for this kid," she whimpered. When the family's modest home was in sight, her little dog ran ahead. Lisa turned the corner, approaching the final squares of sidewalk lining her front yard.

One last time she glanced down at the sidewalk in front of her before heading up the driveway. And there, wedged between some sticks and stones, lay not a one-dollar bill, but a clean, crisp twenty-dollar bill! She couldn't believe her eyes. Grabbing the money, she jumped up and down and screamed for the whole neighborhood to hear, "There is a God! There is a God! There is a God!"

I'll bet she blew a few big bubbles over that one!

Just across the river from where Lisa lived in Portland, Oregon, another ten-year-old had a similar experience. My friend Mary Kae was in Junior Girl Scouts in Skamania, Washington, and her troop trekked to the Stevenson community pool each week for a swim night. Mary Kae was the kind of kid who never left the water once she took the plunge. It didn't matter if she looked like a prune by the end of the evening—she just loved flapping around in the wet stuff.

One Monday morning, Mary Kae reminded her mom about swim night and asked for ten cents so she could enter the pool. Money was tight for their family during those years, and there wasn't a dime for anything but the bare necessities. Knowing how much the activity meant to Mary Kae, her mother said, "Let's pray about this and ask God to provide a dime. If He wants you to go tonight, He will make a way."

The family prayed together after breakfast, and Mary Kae went to school. She didn't think much about the evening events during classes. But on the way home, she was hoping with all of her heart that her mom would have a dime when she walked in the door. When she was about halfway home, her daydreams were suddenly interrupted. Several feet ahead of her on the sidewalk was something shiny, reflecting the sunlight like a mirror. A few steps later, Mary Kae discovered a dime, an answered prayer, and a lesson she tucked away in her heart for the rest of her days.

I felt like I'd just downed a double mocha after my friends told me their stories. With my faith energized, I thought, I want my kids to hear these stories. Better yet, I want them to have stories of their own.

I started asking my children more frequently, to identify their concrete needs so we could pray for them and give our family more opportunities to witness God's faithfulness. The lists grew over time, including simple things such as finding misplaced homework assignments, Nathan's lost coat, and Ben's missing shoes. We prayed for the return of lost luggage after a trip, healing for ill friends, and restoration for broken relationships. Many of the requests I logged in my prayer journal, and it bolstered our faith to cross items off the list when the prayers were answered. Some requests we're still waiting on…which is teaching us patience.

Children love to hear their moms and dads tell stories. Why not create some new family stories of your own? Find out what your children are concerned about and help them bring their requests to the Lord. Share some ways God has met your needs to bolster their faith. Like Lisa and Mary Kae, your children will cherish these lessons for a lifetime. Nothing is too insignificant or too small to bring to God in prayer.

Power Perk: A Taste of Humor

My friend Lynn told me that when her husband, Bob, came home from work recently, he opened the front door and walked into total bedlam. Their three-year-old was running around without a stitch of clothing, and smears of chocolate were swirled in patterns over her hands, face, and belly. The kitchen looked like a disaster area with dishes and pans everywhere. The peanut butter jar was open, on its side, with blobs of the gooey substance all over the counter. A sour smell wafted from the milk carton on the table, and potato chips crunched under Bob's feet as he ventured further into the kitchen.

The bathroom faucet roared full blast, and mountains of toothpaste protruded from the mirror. Not a bed was made. Not a toy was picked up. Not a toilet was flushed. Not a piece of dirty clothing was in the hamper. Not a book was on the shelf. Not a Cheerio was in the box—in fact, a string of little O's snaked from the kitchen to the living room.

Fearing that something had happened to Lynn, Bob began to search for her throughout the house. Much to his surprise, he found her sitting on the back deck in a lounge chair, greased with Coppertone and soaking in the sun.

"Welcome home!" Lynn said with a smile when Bob opened the French doors.

"Are you okay?" he asked.

"Yes, I'm fine," she responded calmly. "Just enjoying some R and R."

Confused, Bob said, "What happened here today?"

With a twinkle in her eye, Lynn replied, "Every day when you come home from work, you ask me what I did all day. Well, today I just didn't do it."

CHAPTER 12

Accepting a New Destination

I have learned to be content, whatever the circumstances may be. I know how to live when things are difficult and I know how to live when things are prosperous. In general and in particular I have learned the secret of... facing either plenty or poverty. I am ready for anything through the strength of the One who lives within me."

—Philippians 4:11–13, *Phillips*

When Nathan was born with Down Syndrome, cards and letters poured in from family and friends. They wanted to help and share in our grief. One letter contained a newspaper clipping that challenged me to open my heart to the new direction my life had taken. I realized that much of my anguish was caused by my own resistance.

Being in a tug-of-war with the events or circumstances in our lives does not change things. What is, *is*. Trying to escape the situation or deny reality doesn't help either. But I know something that does help.

Acceptance.

Acceptance doesn't make things harder, it makes things easier. It empowers us to see with a new set of eyes. Emily Perl Kingsley said it beautifully in a little story she penned years ago.

I am often asked to describe the experience of raising a child with a disability—to try to help people who have not shared that unique experience to understand it, to imagine how it would feel. It's like this…

When you're going to have a baby, it's like planning a fabulous vacation trip to Italy. You buy a bunch of guide books and make your wonderful plans. The Coliseum. The Michelangelo David. The gondolas in Venice. You may learn some handy phrases in Italian. It's all very exciting.

After months of eager anticipation, the day finally arrives. You pack your bags and off you go. Several hours later, the plane lands. The stewardess comes in and says, "Welcome to Holland."

"Holland?!?" you say. "What do you mean Holland? I signed up for Italy! I'm supposed to be in Italy. All my life I've dreamed of going to Italy."

But there's been a change in the flight plan. They've landed in Holland and there you must stay.

The important thing is that they haven't taken you to a horrible, disgusting, filthy place, full of pestilence, famine and disease. It's just a different place.

So you must go out and buy new guide books. And you must learn a whole new language. And you will meet a whole new group of people you would never have met.

It's just a different place. It's slower-paced than Italy, less flashy than Italy. But after you've been there for a while and you catch your breath, you look around…and you begin to notice that Holland has windmills…and Holland has tulips. Holland even has Rembrandts.

But everyone you know is busy coming and going from Italy…and they're all bragging about what a wonderful time they had there. And for the rest of your life, you will say, "Yes, that's where I was supposed to go. That's what I had planned."

And the pain of that will never, ever, ever, *ever* go away…because the loss of that dream is a very very significant loss.

But…if you spend your life mourning the fact that you didn't get to Italy, you may never be free to enjoy the very special, the very lovely things…about Holland.[1]

I had occasion to think about that "unintended Holland trip" when I found myself sitting at a preschool classroom table with my knees in my throat. (Preschool chairs are not made for adult women five-feet-seven-inches tall!) But the uncomfortable seating didn't matter. This was a special occasion—Nathan had invited me to a Mother's Day tea.

It had been years since I attended my first celebration as a mom. I remember watching little Jessie, adorable in her pink polka-dot dress and blond ponytail, sing at a school Mother's Day performance. With utmost confidence, she stood in the front row and belted out the songs at the top of her lungs. Watching her perform, I thought, *She's so bubbly and full of life. None of this intimidates her.*

Then there was the time Ben played Joseph in the kindergarten Christmas program. He was given the assignment of pulling Mary several times around stage inside a cardboard donkey, which the little girl carried around her waist. This was supposed to represent their long journey to Bethlehem.

The teacher had told them to park the donkey stage left before walking over to the manger, stage right. When Ben-Joseph tugged on the rope to park the donkey as per instructions, however, he hit a snag. Mary, with a mind of her own, assertively leaned back in her donkey, refusing to budge. But Joseph was a man on a mission and wasn't about to be bullied. So he hauled off and gave a fierce yank on the rope...which propelled a startled Mary three feet forward. Infuriated, Mary threw down her donkey, planted her hands on her hips, gave Joseph a dirty look, and stomped off stage.

So much for an angelic nativity scene. Joseph, stunned by Mary's unpredictable mood swing, trod over to the manger and arranged his face in a huge pout. And so goes the story of Mary and Joseph's first fight.

There were many times I watched Jessie and Ben on stage and laughed and cried, old softy that I am. Seeing them perform made me one proud mom. After the formal presentations, they usually served me coffee and cookies and guided me around the classroom to see the things they had made for the occasion. They were proud I had come and proud I was their mother.

With Nathan, I knew it would be different.

This time it would be Holland, not Italy.

Nathan was the only child in the class with a handicap. I knew he wouldn't be able to articulate the words of the songs, and he'd probably miss some hand motions. I knew the twenty other mothers in the classroom would upset his predictable routine and shake his confidence. I wasn't sure at all how the morning would go…but I made an important decision before I ever walked through that classroom door: I decided to open my heart to whatever lay ahead—and to accept it with gratitude.

Acceptance is powerful. It brings quiet peace to a heart torn with conflict. It comes when we make a simple choice to take a deep breath and say, "I am exactly where I'm supposed to be at this moment in time." It means we stop wasting precious time and emotional energy wishing things were different, or longing to be someone else, or wanting another set of circumstances. It's a force for change that can turn bad into good. It's the door to joy and contentment. It's trusting that "My times are in your hands" (Psalm 31:15).

It doesn't matter what the circumstance. It may be singleness. Or widowhood. Or a heartbreaking marriage. Or infertility. Or disability. Or lingering illness. Or any life situation in which we find ourselves powerless, helpless, and unable to effect change. With Paul, we learn to say, "I have learned the secret of being content in any and every situation" (Philippians 4:12).

And not just content, but truly thankful.

When the children presented their songs at tea time, Nathan stood at my side and made his best effort to say a few syllables. His hand motions weren't well defined, but they were consistent. His pudgy little hand gripped my shirt, and he smiled much of the time. He was enjoying this! During one of the songs, I glanced at another mom who happened to be watching Nathan. She had sad tears in her eyes. I'm not sure what she was thinking, but a spontaneous insight bubbled to the surface as I witnessed this event.

Yes, I was in a "different place," not one of my choosing. That much was clear. But I also realized that God was in this different place and that He had brought me here.

After the presentation, I took Nathan by the hand and guided him around the room to view his artwork on the walls. I pointed to his pictures and said, "Very nice, Nathan!" And then he proceeded to bring me one cookie after another from the silver tray. Between the two of us, we must have eaten a dozen. The limit was two. Oh, well.

I felt a deep sense of gratitude when I left the school that day—gratitude to God for helping me move through years of grief toward acceptance.

That doesn't mean I don't feel sad now and then. I do.

That doesn't mean I never play the "what if" game. I do.

That doesn't mean I never daydream about "Italy." I do.

But those wistful, longing thoughts and feelings come less frequently now.

I am grateful that God has taught our family to perceive Nathan's differences as uniquenesses to be appreciated and understood. I am grateful that the joy over what Nathan can do far surpasses the sadness over what he cannot do. But most of all, I am grateful that God has given "the handicapped boy in the class" (as some refer to him) to me and that he's proud I'm his mom.

There's a lot of love in Holland.[2]

Power Perk: A Taste of Hope

"I know, O Lord, that a man's life is not his own; it is not for man to direct his steps."

—Jeremiah 10:23

"God is an ever-present Spirit guiding all that happens to a wise and holy end."

—David Hume[1]

"God leads us step by step, from event to event. Only afterward, as we look back over the way we have come and reconsider certain important moments in our lives in the light of all that has followed them, or when we survey the whole progress of our lives, do we experience the feeling of having been led without knowing it, the feeling that God has mysteriously guided us."

—Paul Tournier[2]

"There are in everyone's life certain connections, twists, and turns which pass a while under the category of chance, but at the last, well examined, prove to be the very hand of God."

—Sir Thomas Brown[3]

"A man's steps are directed by the Lord."

—Proverbs 20:24

CHAPTER 13
Double Blessing

or the LORD *is good and his love endures forever; his faithfulness continues through all generations."*

—Psalm 100:5

For many years, John and I have had the privilege of serving the people of East Hill Church under the leadership of senior pastor Dr. Ted Roberts and his wife, Diane. They have encouraged us in many ways, but one thing about this dynamic duo stands out to me. Both of their children, Nikki and Brian, are outstanding, well-adjusted young adults who are happily married and gifted contributors in their respective fields. Through the years, we've laughed over the funny stories Ted has told about them from the platform (only with a signed release by Diane and the kids, of course). Recently, Diane told me about a series of events from Nikki's life that left me smiling about God's incredible faithfulness.

Sending Nikki off to college was not an easy assignment for Diane. It's hard for parents to let go of those they love. But in a unique way, God showed Ted and Diane that He was guiding and directing their daughter as she moved out from under their care.

Nikki has always been a responsible child, and she's worked hard to help pay for her college education. In the spring prior to her sophomore year, she wrote a letter to her parents asking for advice. The previous summer, Nikki had worked as a firefighter and earned six thousand dollars in three and a half months. She was planning to take the same job the following summer. But there was a glitch. A friend had asked her to help lead a junior high camp during June and July. The wages during those two months would cover only her expenses to and from camp. She was concerned the forestry service wouldn't hire her if she couldn't start promptly in June when school ended.

Ted and Diane encouraged Nikki to ask God to show her what He wanted her to do and to check with the forestry service about starting in mid-July. Because of the reputation she had developed as a hard worker, she was given the okay to begin work in the middle of the summer. Half of the problem was solved. But Nikki still needed to figure out how she was going to make enough money to cover her school expenses.

Her parents again encouraged her to seek God's wisdom. They felt certain that if God wanted her to work at the camp, He would provide the money she needed for school. Nikki sensed God was directing her to work with the younger girls that summer, so she made plans to spend seven weeks at camp. It was a great time of fun and spiritual growth for Nikki and the junior highers she counseled.

Camp ended amid heartwarming hugs and tears, and Nikki headed for her next job with the forestry service. When she arrived, she learned that her crew had already left on an assignment. But a new crew was being assembled because of multiple fires blazing in the Northwest. As it turned out, the crew Nikki joined was on constant duty, which meant the money she earned far exceeded what she had planned. Nikki pocketed eight thousand dollars that summer—

more money than she'd earned the summer before and in a shorter amount of time.

But the story isn't over yet. Two years later, the results of Nikki's obedience to God's leading continued to reap rewards. Nikki was newly married and the sole breadwinner while her husband finished his last year of college. They lived in a small college town, where there was an overabundance of qualified students and not enough jobs to go around. She heard about a job opening that seemed to fit her educational background and decided to apply, along with scores of eager collegiates. Many of the applicants were more qualified and more experienced than she was. Nikki had another strike against her. She felt compelled to inform the interviewer that she could only commit to one year of employment because she and her husband planned to move after his graduation.

Much to her astonishment, Nikki got the job. After settling into her new assignment, she mustered the courage to ask why the boss had chosen her. Rather matter-of-factly, he explained, "I noticed on your application that you were a junior high leader at a Christian camp. Our church supports that camp. I knew instantly you were the one I wanted."

None of us knows what lies ahead for our children. But like Ted and Diane discovered, God has wonderful gifts for our kids along the way. There are delightful surprises perfectly planned and perfectly timed just for them. Finding direction in life isn't a do-it-yourself task. Our children are being guided. As they seek God, His plan will unfold in their lives. We can look forward to their future with confidence and certainty that they are safe under God's protective wing.

Power Perk: A Sip of Humor

In biology class, the professor projected a slide of a handsome young man relaxing in the tall grass of a magnificent hillside. Speaking to a roomful of premed students, he pointed to the slide and said, "If you study hard here and in medical school, work even more during your residency, and become the most sought-after physician in a hospital, this can be your kid."[1]

"Children have never been very good at listening to their elders, but they have never failed to imitate them."

—James Baldwin[2]

"Those people who think of adolescence as a happy, carefree time either possess deficient emotions or inadequate memories."

—Louis Bromfield[3]

CHAPTER 14

It's Just a Matter of Time

N *either he who plants nor he who waters is anything, but only God, who makes things grow."*

—1 Corinthians 3:7

During our family's second missions trip to Mexico, we were introduced to Alberto and Claudia, a dynamic couple who pastor two churches on the Baja Peninsula.

Alberto's tattoos first caught my attention. As we approached the tent where church services were held, his shirt was off, and we could see his "body art." I'd never seen so many designs on one body before—snakes, pentagrams, evil eyes, and other ominous images were etched up and down his arms, back, and chest. Every square inch of his torso was covered. I wondered how many hours of needling he endured to make his statement.

When we got closer, Alberto quickly slipped on his shirt, extended his hand, and welcomed us with the warmth and favor of a long-lost relative. Before we knew it, this big lug of a guy was embracing us and bellowing, "Gracias, Dios! Gracias, Dios!" The bold satanic symbols branded on his skin paled in comparison to the overpowering love emanating from this man.

As a therapist, I'm always interested in hearing why and how people change. What catalyzes growth? What makes a positive difference and enhances healing? I knew Alberto had much to teach me from the sharp contrast I saw between his foreboding appearance and his radiant heart.

It had been years since Alberto had shared his past with anyone. He preferred to focus forward—perhaps to avoid dredging up painful memories, or perhaps to preserve his dignity and protect himself from modern-day Pharisees, who would peer down their noses at him. Whatever the case, I'm grateful he opened his dinner table to our family for fish tacos and a story none of us will ever forget. With the help of an interpreter, the tale unfolded.

At the age of five, Alberto knew full well that his father wanted little to do with him. The oldest brother was the chosen favorite. Alberto had three older sisters who could have nurtured him, but he knew nothing of their love. Forming a coalition against him, they made Alberto the brunt of their jokes, the target of their taunts, the aim of their abuse.

His parents labored long and hard—twelve-hour days, seven days a week—to keep food on the table. After work, they were too tired to interact with the children and usually told Alberto to be quiet and go away. How do you quantify the pain of such perpetual rejection? Being a good little boy, Alberto frequently disappeared and went to visit other family members nearby.

"A large prison was located a few streets from our home," Alberto said. "Two of my uncles were behind bars for murder. When I was six years old, I started visiting them every day. They were nice to me and gave me money to buy them food, cigarettes, and other stuff. Whenever I returned, they were glad to see me. I decided prison was a good place because they liked me there and wanted me to come back."

During adolescence, when Alberto's friends were begging their parents to loosen curfews, Alberto was railroading the family rules by sneaking out of the house in the middle of the night. Older friends initiated him into the drug scene. He smoked pot, sniffed glue, and popped amphetamines—anything to get high. Jewelry stolen from his mother's dresser drawer supported his habit.

Alberto couldn't remember all the times he had landed in juvenile jail between the ages of twelve and seventeen. That segment of his life was a blur. But he did recall that after one too many crimes, the juvenile center refused to take him, so he was sent to an adult lockdown facility. Even though he was the youngest inmate, the guards pegged him as one of the meanest. At twenty-one, he was sentenced to twenty-seven years in prison for drug trafficking and instigating prison riots.

"The guards hated me," he recalled. "The prisoners hated me. And I hated them. I provoked fights and pulled knives on inmates to coerce them into giving me their money so I could turn drug deals. Sometimes it worked, but not always. That's when the gang brawls broke out. During one incident, I cut out an inmate's left eye and sliced off the fingers of his right hand. He and his friends retaliated one night, attacking me with knives and clubs when I was asleep."

The gang left Alberto for dead. But it wasn't time for him to meet his maker. Twenty-two knife holes were found in Alberto's sleeping bag, but his flesh was penetrated only twice—once under his arm and once in his back.

Unrest ruled the prison. The head of security wanted to end Alberto's toxic influence on the other inmates, so he transferred him to a secured mental hospital, where he was diagnosed schizophrenic and treated with multiple medications. For five years, a psychiatrist treated him with a variety of medical interventions to no avail. He didn't know that Alberto's satanic worship rituals were energizing his evil ways. The doctor tried his best to help, but one afternoon while he and Alberto were talking, Alberto flew into a rage, grabbed the doctor by the throat, and threw him against the wall. It took several guards to restrain Alberto. The mental hospital washed their hands of him, and Alberto was transferred to Isles Marias, otherwise known as Mary's Island, off the coast of Mexico.

It's an island known to Hispanics as hell on earth, reserved strictly for the most hard-core criminals. Alberto's tainted reputation preceded him. The authorities didn't want any troublemakers in their camp, and to prove their point they assigned Alberto to eighteen months in solitary confinement the moment he stepped off the boat and onto the island. In the darkness of his ten-by-ten-foot hole in the ground, Alberto's mind started playing tricks on him. He heard and saw things he knew weren't there. The doctors called it auditory and visual hallucinations. Alberto simply thought he was losing his mind.

In time, a man from Los Angeles who had a burden for those behind bars came to the prison. He had heard about "the man in solitary," and he asked to see Alberto. Under close scrutiny, this white man entered his cell, and the first words out of his mouth were, "Alberto, God loves you."

Alberto cursed in the man's face. But after the man left, something inside snapped. It was the first time in Alberto's life he had ever heard that anyone loved him. A tiny seed of hope slipped it's way into a crack in Alberto's heart that day.

During the next six months in solitary, Alberto replayed the man's words over and over in his mind: "Alberto, God loves you…God loves you." As the seed took root, the hallucinations went away. Eventually, Alberto was allowed to join the other prisoners.

Life on the island was torture. Alberto worked hard labor fifteen hours a day, splitting rocks and hauling bags of salt. Many prisoners died in the 125-degree heat. When the rock salt burned Alberto's blistered feet and back, death would have been a welcome reprieve. The only moments of relief came midday when Alberto tended to the livestock on the island. Anything was better than those backbreaking hours, hammering boulders under the scorching sun.

One afternoon while Alberto was walking from one building to the next, he heard singing. It wasn't an auditory hallucination this time. It was a Bible study and worship service. He craned his neck to peer through the crowd and there, standing in front of the prisoners, was the man who had visited Alberto in solitary confinement. He paused and listened to the man tell a story about a prodigal son who was estranged from his father, living in a pigpen. Alberto thought the man was talking about him. He hadn't talked to his father in years, and the pigs on the island were his responsibility.

In one earth-stopping moment, Alberto's whole life flashed before him. All the drugs. Fights. Stealing. Lies. Hatred. Rage. And the five year-old little boy who had laid awake at night, dreaming of becoming a biologist.

Alberto had never cried a tear in his life, but thirty years' worth of dammed-up emotions exploded through his defenses, and he wept convulsively. It was all he could do to make his way through the crowd to talk with the man in front. He knew he desperately needed this man's God of love.

The preacher got down on his knees with Alberto and helped him say a simple prayer to confess his wrongs and seek God's forgiveness. On a blistering 125-degree day, an angry young man knelt behind barbed wire, in a place known as hell on earth, and God deposited a taste of heaven in his heart and set a prisoner free.

For eighteen years, Alberto had been hooked on uppers and downers, powders and pills. You name it, he did it. But that afternoon, everything changed. The desire for drugs disappeared.

The cravings stopped. The temptations died.

"It was like my heart caught fire!" Alberto exclaimed.

Oh, a fire blazed all right, but much different from before. Flames of rage had been doused, and now his heart burned with a passion to tell other inmates about the God he had encountered. During the months that followed, Alberto told every prisoner who would listen about God's love. Then, unexpectedly, the director of the prison called Alberto into his office.

"I don't know what you are doing, Alberto, but things are getting better in the prison," he said. "What can I do to help you?"

"I want to help the other men find God," Alberto enthusiastically responded.

"So what do you need?"

"I need chairs and a meeting room."

His requests were granted, and in 1990 Alberto started a Bible study that is still going strong in the prison today. But the director wasn't as altruistic as you might think. He took advantage of Alberto's peace-making powers and falsified bad reports about him to government authorities in Mexico City. He planned to keep Alberto on the island as long as possible because it made his job easier.

Nevertheless, God was bigger than the conniving director, and His plans for Alberto prevailed. It was just a matter of time.

A team of psychiatrists conducted annual evaluations of the inmates. The doctors spent fifteen minutes with each person. But Alberto's quarter-hour session turned into four hours as the psychiatrist assigned to his case wept through the story of a transformed man. The final evaluation conflicted with the prison director's reports.

Shortly thereafter, the government transferred the prison director to another job. The man who replaced him heard about Alberto's model behavior from prison guards. Curious about this too-good-to-be-true individual, he requested a meeting. When Alberto walked through the official's doorway, he was surprised to discover that he recognized the man sitting behind the desk. It was the judge who sentenced Alberto to juvenile jail the very first time.

The judge remembered the hardened twelve-year-old from years before. He recalled the hatred in the youngster's eyes and was amazed by the changes he saw in Alberto. Alberto's transformation made such a dramatic impact on the new director that he purchased an airline ticket with his own money and flew to Mexico City to campaign for Alberto's release. In 1993, Alberto walked out of prison, thirteen years ahead of schedule.

No more hammering boulders or dragging chains for this man. Now he's hammering the gates of hell and helping to break the chains of darkness for anyone who seeks his help. God has replaced his cold, hard stares with tearful eyes of compassion. He's a hoodlum turned hero. A rioter turned righteous. A misdiagnosed "schizophrenic" transformed into a stable man, skilled in the ways of the Spirit.

Few men work as hard and with as much passion for God as Alberto. We chuckled when he told us one of his churches holds services in a room underneath the police department. The policemen who work upstairs picked up Alberto numerous times when he was a teenage rebel. When Alberto sees his former arresters in the parking lot, he smiles and says, "I'm saving a chair for you in church." The officers haven't visited yet, but they refer all their "problem" arrests to Alberto.

That night over fish tacos, we learned how a tiny seed of hope planted in faith and watered by the Spirit can bloom and grow against all odds. Miracles happen today. Those in the dark are walking into the light. Those bound by the shackles of black magic and witchcraft are being liberated. Marriages and families are being restored. It's true for Alberto and for the many families he serves in Mexico. Alberto gives total credit to God, not social systems or rehab programs. Community-based professional services aren't affordable for most families in his country. But what Alberto has to offer his people, money can't buy. You can't put a price tag on the healing power of God.

Alberto has made amends with many from his past. Several years ago, he tracked down the man he blinded and maimed on the island. With tearful regret, he apologized and asked the man for forgiveness. Somehow that man found the wherewithal to grant his request.

Alberto has helped many begin their spiritual journey, but one of his greatest joys came the night Alberto's father told him he wanted to know his God. Despite the work God is doing in his father, Alberto has never heard him say, "I love you." Expressing affection doesn't come easy in his family. But God continues to help Alberto grow beyond his weaknesses. The Spirit of God is showing him how to break unhealthy family patterns. Just last month Alberto did something he had never done before. He hugged his own boy and for the first time said, "I love you, son."

Alberto's story is a powerful reminder that in God's economy we don't have to be products of our past. And neither do our children. Even though we, as parents, have made mistakes along the way, we can still plant seeds of truth in our kids' hearts today. We can nourish and protect those seeds with prayer, and then trust the Spirit of God to do His part. Growth is inevitable. It may not come as quickly as we would like, but it will come.

Moms and dads, keep sowing those seeds. Ask God to place people in your children's lives who will sow along with you. And then keep the faith. God is the one who makes things grow. He is faithful.

Power Perk: A Taste of Hope

"The Bible teaches—and Christian experience abundantly confirms—that the works of the Holy Spirit are unpredictable and by no means confined to the institutional church. Even the most narrow-minded Christian must admit, on occasion, that the Holy Spirit seems to be working in and through people who do not consciously profess faith in Christ. This should not surprise anyone who has read the New Testament. Jesus was always consorting with sinners, to the horror of pious types who thought he should have been exclusively concerned with them."

—Louis Cassels[1]

"In the last days, God says, I will pour out my Spirit on all people. Your sons and daughters will prophesy, your young men will see visions, your old men will dream dreams. Even on my servants, both men and women, I will pour out my Spirit in those days, and they will prophesy."

—Acts 2:17–18

"The Holy Spirit does not obliterate a man's personality; he lifts it to its highest use."

—Oswald Chambers[2]

CHAPTER 15
Talk Show Tales

I know that you can do all things; no plan of yours can be thwarted."
—Job 42:2

It was my first trip abroad for an international television broadcast to promote my book *Angel Behind the Rocking Chair*. And I was excited. The program was part of a Mother's Day celebration series. The Christian station had invited me to talk about the joys and challenges of raising three children, one with Down Syndrome.

I hugged and kissed the kids as they went off to school, asked them to pray for me, and then headed for the airport. The trip seemed simple enough. Portland to Cincinnati. Cincinnati to Toronto. No problem. It was a nice plan. Four and a half hours of leisurely reading time with no interruptions. That is, unless I pushed the little orange call button to request a fresh refill of coffee from a friendly stewardess. Airplane coffee isn't the best, and Styrofoam cups fall short of my fancy mugs, but I don't complain when I don't have to brew it, someone else is pouring, and I can sip it as slowly as I want!

Peculiar things happen during travel. There I was, engulfed in reading one of my favorite books, when something across the aisle caught my attention. The lady in the seat across from me reached up and pushed the orange call button. That wasn't unusual, but what happened next borders on…well, I'll just call it amusing. This woman, evidently new to air travel, proceeded to rise from her seat and speak into the little orange button. She must have assumed it was a two-way speaker, like the ones you find at drive-thru food joints. With assertive gusto, she said, "I'd like someone to bring me a Coca-Cola, please!" Then she sat down.

I quickly buried my face in a Kleenex, pretending to cough and blow my nose, so she wouldn't see me giggling. A steward happened to be standing nearby and didn't miss the opportunity for some fun. Picking up the microphone, he called over the loud speaker, "Ma'am, would you like French fries with your Coke?" Without hesitation, the woman pushed the orange button again, stood to speak directly into it, and politely said, "No, thank you." By this time, everyone within viewing distance realized what was going on and split a gut laughing for the next fifty miles.

As soon as the wheels touched down in Toronto, I made a beeline for baggage claim. I wanted to get to the hotel as fast as possible so I could soak in the hot tub to calm my talk show jitters. After the soak, I'd have a quiet hour to mentally prepare for the next morning before turning out the lights. A good night's sleep was top priority.

Oh, well, it was a nice plan. All too soon it began to crumble. As it turned out, passing through customs was not a speedy or pleasant process. The declaration form asked if I was traveling for business or personal reasons. I checked business. It also asked if I was carrying any commercial products. Being a good, honest citizen, I checked, "Yes." That flagged the customs officials, who asked me to step aside and wait…and wait…and wait.

I had cases of books with me for an author autographing party after the television show, and they wanted to know exactly how many I had, the cost, and so on. Apparently they didn't trust my truthful-looking face and instructed me to open the boxes so they could take an exact count of the inventory. I spent an hour and a half in customs, with someone who could barely speak English, counting books, only to be told I owed them big bucks for "goods and services tax." So much for soaking away my tension in the hot tub.

Toward the end of that disturbing detour, I was not feeling particularly nice. As I looked at the not-so-friendly foreign agent across from me, I thought, *I wish I had lied on that form. I should have checked "no commercial goods." I could be praying and meditating right now if it weren't for this bozo hassling me.* I know, the logic wasn't even close to rational. Eventually, I snapped out of it and asked God to forgive me for my stinkin' thinkin'.

By the time I reached the hotel, it was past 11:00 P.M., and the manager was alone at the front desk. For such a lovely hotel, it was woefully understaffed. So guess who got to carry all of her luggage and cases of books to her room without assistance? Ah, the perks of being a published author.

A hot shower eased my aggravation, and with a sigh of relief, I climbed into bed and pulled the covers up close, thanked the Lord for a safe if tiring journey, and gratefully anticipated seven full hours of sleep before reveille.

Oh, well, it was a nice plan. At 2:32 A.M., I was startled awake by a sharp pain just under my left eyebrow. I reached up to feel my face and discovered a Canadian spider had decided to make my American flesh his midnight snack. I swatted the rude intruder and rolled over to go back to sleep. No such luck. My adrenaline had already kicked in, and the lights were on in my brain. For the next two hours, I watched the bright red digital lights on the clock radio click away. I finally dozed off sometime after 4:30 A.M., until a wake-up call jolted me from my slumber.

Fumbling my way to the bathroom, I turned on the hot water, grabbed a washcloth, and glanced up to find an unsightly reflection staring at me in the mirror. Bloodshot eyes and a large, red bump under my left brow were not what I wanted to see! That spider had feasted in the middle of the night. And the spot that hungry bug bit looked like a big honking zit. I felt pity for the poor makeup artist at the studio. She had her work cut out for her.

To top it off, I realized—after my steaming shower—that I had forgotten my deodorant and the picks for my electric curlers. "Oh, great," I winced. "I'm going on national TV with BO, flat hair, and a zit-like bite on my eye." My confidence was dwindling.

I did my best to blow-dry and spray my hair into shape, and I spritzed on a few extra sprays of perfume—just in case. Banking on the studio's makeup artist to transform me, I set out for a hearty breakfast and prep time for the interview.

Jamie, my waitress, was a sweet Canadian, whose cheery smile put me at ease. I must have looked like I needed some coffee because she never even bothered to ask. She just started pouring.

"Cream?" she asked politely.

"Yes, please," I responded.

Jamie placed a small bowl of creamers on the table and went about her business. As I peeled back the foil on a container of creamer, my silk nail popped off three-fourths of the way back to the cuticle, landing smack dab in the middle of that wonderful java. All I could do was laugh.

Well, I thought, *now I'm going to the studio with BO, flat hair, and a nubby stub.*

The studio had given explicit instructions about nail care to prevent any distractions during the interview. Since I didn't have any nail glue with me, I figured I'd have to sit on my right hand during the TV spot so I didn't flash my stub.

I showed Jamie my woes, and she proceeded to give me a step-by-step lesson on how to open a creamer without breaking a nail. Taking my knife from the table, she jabbed it through the center of the foil lid and twisted. I thought, *Where was this resourceful person last night when I needed her in customs?*

At the station, I was introduced to a wonderful crew, who escorted me to the greenroom. There, the friendly makeup woman went to work on the "the project of the year." It was amazing to see the finished product. No more zit. No more stub. I had retrieved my nail from my coffee, and she had some nail glue in her bag of tricks. The greenroom was stocked with electric curlers that were hot and ready for use. My transformation was nearly complete.

I was feeling upbeat about everything until I overheard another author featured on the program say to the talk show host, "I meant to tell you that my books have sold over a million copies."

I sank into my seat. *Oh, dear,* I thought. *I hope they don't ask me how many copies my books have sold. I wouldn't know what to tell them. But one thing I know for sure—it's not a million copies.* Fortunately, they never asked.

With show time approaching quickly, all the guests and staff joined together in the greenroom for prayer. We asked God to encourage moms and dads who were troubled about their children. We prayed for the telephone counselors, asking God to use them in strategic ways as they spoke with those seeking help. And we prayed that God would impart a new measure of faith, courage, and strength to those who were weary.

Then we were quiet. No one said a word. A gentle hush

descended in that little room. God's presence was unmistakable. I sensed the compassionate ache in His heart for bruised and broken people—the lost, those who needed answers, parents who needed peace. My heart ached with His heart. Tears fell.

At that moment, nothing else mattered to me. It didn't matter if I looked good. It didn't matter if I smelled good. It didn't matter if I had been uncomfortable or inconvenienced. It didn't matter how many of my books sold over the air. What mattered was God's desire to release His healing touch on troubled souls. Everything else was incidental.

I knew some in the viewing audience were walking through the same valley of the shadow we had trod when we learned Nathan had Down Syndrome. More than anything, I wanted God to take the words the host and I exchanged and breathe fresh hope into weary hearts.

I wanted moms and dads to know that getting beyond their pain doesn't take trying harder. It takes trust—trust in the one who can take even our disappointments, unmet expectations, and heartbreaks and weave them together with wisdom to accomplish His purposes in our lives. Nothing can thwart His plans. Nothing.

I left the television station that day sensing God was pleased— our mission was accomplished. On the return trip, getting through customs was a breeze. After all, I knew my way around, and they already had my money. After a quick stop at the duty-free shop to buy a bottle of my favorite perfume, which was most helpful after sitting under hot studio lights, I made my way to the gate. I was eager to get back to Portland to spend the evening with my family and tuck my children into bed.

Oh, well, it was a nice plan. When I arrived at the gate, I had to wait...and wait...and wait. What began as a half-hour delay turned into two hours, which prevented me from making my connection in Cincinnati. The airline rerouted me to Atlanta—another two-hour delay—so I could catch a plane to the West Coast.

But not all was lost. Because of the inconvenience, I was bumped up to first class. I enjoyed a lovely grilled bass dinner followed by a hot fudge sundae, decked with toppings galore. The steward assured me they had removed the calories before takeoff.

After the meal, I grabbed a book, leaned back, and made myself comfortable under two little blue blankets. There were some extra perks, too. As I nourished my soul with reflections of God's goodness, the steward kept a fresh pot of decaf brewing all the way home. I didn't have to request refills by pushing the little orange call button. And the cream came in a small white pitcher, minus a peel-back foil lid

Power Perk: A Sip of Humor

A kindergarten-aged girl went with her mother to a wedding ceremony. The little girl was wide eyed as she watched the bride walk down the aisle in her beautiful gown. When the bride reached the front of the church, the girl tugged on her mother's skirt and asked, "Mommy, why is the bride wearing all white?"

The mother thought for a moment and said, "White represents happiness. This is the happiest day of her life."

That seemed to satisfy the little girl for a while, but a few minutes later she turned to her mother and whispered, "Mommy, why is the groom wearing only black?"

A letter written by a parent to a teacher:

My son is under doctor's care and should not take fiscal ed. Please execute him.

Sincerely,
Mrs. Whiteall[1]

A letter written by a parent to a county department:

I am very annoyed that you have branded my son illiterate. This is a dirty lie, as I was married a week before he was born.

Sincerely,
Mrs. Maken[2]

CHAPTER 16

The Battle Belongs to the Lord

or our struggle is not against flesh and blood, but against the rulers, against the authorities, against the powers of this dark world and against the spiritual forces of evil in the heavenly realms."

—Ephesians 6:12

A physician in town referred her to me.

"The woman I'm sending you is agoraphobic," he said, using the medical term for the debilitating fear that keeps a person house-bound. "She also has persistent panic attacks and ghoulish flash-backs. I can help her with medication, but she needs therapy."

Cari and I met the following week, and during that first session, the amazing story of her past unfolded.

She was the fifth baby born into a family of six children. Immediately following her birth, her parents dedicated her to Satan. I know what you're thinking. This kind of stuff doesn't happen in America. I wish that were true. Unfortunately, it happens more than anyone in the mental health or legal professions prefers to admit. I share this story with you not to be sensational or overly dramatic. I share it because it is a remarkable testimony of what the Spirit of God can do in a family when He is given an invitation.

Cari was a victim of satanic ritual abuse. Occult ceremonies replete with pornography and perverted sex acts were performed in her home. Children were molested and used as guinea pigs for drug experiments. God was openly blasphemed. On more than one occasion, Cari witnessed her sisters being tied to a cross as a mockery of Christ.

When Cari was three years old, her father died of cancer, leaving behind little money for the family to live on. Food was scarce. As one of the youngest in the clan, Cari found it hard to get her fair share at mealtime. The older children were quicker at grabbing what was dished out. Many nights she went to bed hungry.

Cari's family had convinced her that she was stupid and that she'd never amount to anything. She was a tenderhearted child, who her mother and sisters were determined to "toughen up." They teased her unmercifully. They kept the curtains closed at all times to protect their secrets. They locked the doors and refused to let Cari play with other children. Nosy neighbors were avoided like the plague.

When Cari was nine years old, her mother remarried. They moved into a new home, and for the first time in her life, Cari had a bicycle and good food to eat. But the "honeymoon" ended when her stepfather and half-brother started molesting her. They said their midnight madness was all her fault and threatened to torture her if she breathed a word to anyone. When her mother suspected trouble, Cari denied everything for fear they would lose their home and be thrown out on the streets.

During high school, Cari heard voices in her head that tried to persuade her to use her mental abilities to move objects. "All you have to do is clear your mind and focus," they taunted. Popularity, money, and power were the promised rewards. But the voices scared Cari. Intuitively she knew that evil lurked behind their intentions.

The only "love" she knew was what she found between the

sheets with guys who used her body to satisfy themselves. Sleeping around left her feeling cheap and dirty, so drugs became her friend to numb the pain. That is, until the day she had a bad trip on angel dust. Horrified by thoughts of death, she cried out to God, "If you get me out of this alive, I'll never do drugs again."

She awoke twenty-four hours later in a thick mental fog, unable to recall anything that had happened, except her promise to God. It was the last time she ever used drugs. The cost was high, though, because no one trusted her after that. Her drug-using friends called her a "narc," and the clean kids called her a druggie. How do you measure the despair of a young teen trying to survive with no place to belong and no one to help?

Cari walked the marriage aisle soon after high school graduation. Nine months later, tragedy struck. Her husband went blind. Many nights she cried herself to sleep, begging God to give *her* eyes to her husband. Again, voices taunted her, this time saying her husband's blindness was all her fault. She believed the lies.

Cari and her husband tried their best to make the marriage work for seven years, at least for the sake of the two children they had brought into the world. But the stress, lack of relational skills, and the razor-sharp hooks of pornography shredded their covenant vows. When the divorce was final, Cari packed her bags and walked out the door, leaving her husband and children behind. Her son was eight months old, and her daughter was in grade school. She figured the kids would be better off with their dad since he had a home and stable income from Social Security and wealthy parents who helped financially.

For more than a year, Cari lived in her car, partied every night, and looked for handouts wherever possible. Most of the men she ran with kept her well stocked with alcohol and cigarettes. Every once in a while, they bought her breakfast.

Skipping ahead a few years, Cari remarried with high hopes for new beginnings. But her life soon began to unravel again. Intrusive thoughts plagued her waking hours. Terrorizing nightmares interrupted her sleep. She was constantly struggling to resist an overwhelming pull back to the dark places where the satanic rituals were held when she was a child.

Describing her inner battle, she told me, "It's like demons are dancing around in my head, telling me I'm supposed to be taking care of dead bodies."

These flashbacks invaded with such intensity and frequency that she thought she was losing her mind. She had made an appointment with her doctor, hoping he could silence the voices and end the mind wars. That's when he prescribed medication and referred her to me.

Cari was a woman driven to self-destruction, driven to isolation, driven to desert her precious children, driven to self-mutilate, driven to dark and solitary places among tombs. She was pale. She shook with fear and tapped her foot through the entire session. Her recollections evoked deep emotion in me that I found difficult to shake.

It was clear to me that Cari had taken a scary step forward to seek counseling from a complete stranger. Given her lack of trust in anyone, I was amazed she had the ego strength to follow through with the appointment. I knew she needed time to develop trust in our relationship before she would be able to receive much input. My immediate goal was to listen, learn, and assess her needs to the best of my ability.

We closed the session after forty-five minutes and agreed to meet again in the near future. I grieved for this tormented woman. As she walked out the door, I prayed God's blessing upon her and asked for His help during our future sessions.

As I thought about all Cari had told me, I couldn't help but recall the gospel account in which Jesus crossed paths with the man possessed by demons. I saw so many similarities between the two stories. That evening, I went home and reread the passage in Mark:

> When Jesus got out of the boat, a man with an evil spirit came from the tombs to meet him. This man lived in the tombs, and no one could bind him any more, not even with a chain....
>
> When he saw Jesus from a distance, he ran and fell on his knees in front of him. He shouted at the top of his voice, "What do you want with me, Jesus, Son of the Most High God? Swear to God that you won't torture me!" For Jesus had said to him, "Come out of this man, you evil spirit!"
>
> Then Jesus asked him, "What is your name?"
>
> "My name is Legion," he replied, "for we are many." And he begged Jesus again and again not to send them out of the area.
>
> A large herd of pigs was feeding on the nearby hillside. The demons begged Jesus, "Send us among the pigs; allow us to go into them." He gave them permission, and the evil spirits came out and went into the pigs. The herd, about two thousand in number, rushed down the steep bank into the lake and were drowned...
>
> As Jesus was getting into the boat, the man who had been demon-possessed begged to go with him. Jesus did not let him, but said, "Go home to your family and tell them how much the Lord has done for you, and how he has had mercy on you." So the man went away and began

to tell in the Decapolis how much Jesus had done for him. And all the people were amazed. (5:2–3, 6–13, 18–20)

No one had been able to help this man. From what we're told, human strength couldn't even confine the man long enough for assistance to be offered. The keys of this world could not unlock the door to this man's prison.

I sensed this was true for Cari, too. Yes, she needed counseling to help her learn healthy life skills. But it didn't take much discernment to see that she also needed spiritual assistance if we were going to make progress in therapy. When I had asked about her faith orientation, she told me she didn't go to church, and her husband was opposed to organized religion of any kind. *This is going to be a challenge,* I thought. Little did I know what God had planned for the days ahead.

Cari awoke on a Sunday morning wanting to "hop and shop" garage sales. She had been on medication, which eased her agoraphobia, and she was starting to venture out on her own. She drove to the opposite side of town from where she lived, and while searching for signs leading to the next sale, she passed a church where crowds of people were coming and going. Curious, Cari decided to stop and investigate. She figured what her husband didn't know wouldn't hurt him. Making her way into the sanctuary, she quietly slipped into a seat in the back row, hoping no one had noticed.

Cari felt agitated through the service but stayed because she wanted to hear more about this God who the preacher said loved her. Two days later, she drove back across town again, walked into the church office, and asked for help with her flashbacks. The secretary contacted one of the church's female counselors, who listened and prayed with her. Some relief came, but the flashbacks continued.

Several days later, she returned to the church again, weary of the mental anguish. The counselor she had seen was on vacation, so she was referred to the pastor on call, who happened to be John Vredevelt, my husband. She didn't know that. She was simply introduced to a man named John.

John greeted Cari and noticed she was unusually fidgety and nervous.

"Can you tell me what you're struggling with?" John asked.

"I have never felt peace," she said softly, wringing her hands and staring at the floor.

While listening to Cari, John discerned the presence of evil powers oppressing her. The Spirit of God prompted him to ask her to read aloud from the Scriptures. He handed her a Bible and pointed to some verses about God's peace. After reading one sentence, Cari slammed the Bible shut and shoved her chair away from him. Her hands curled like claws, and she appeared to be in great pain. With her head turned away and eyes closed tightly, she reared back in her chair and cried, "I can't do anymore! I can't do anymore!"

John prayed and asked Cari if she wanted to be freed from the mental torment. He described steps she could take to receive God's help. Desperate for relief, she asked John if he would help her pray. With his assistance, Cari invited the Spirit of the living God to establish His presence within her and commanded the evil powers that had gained entrance into her life to leave.

An hour and a half later, their time together ended. Cari no longer shook. Her body was relaxed. Color returned to her face. She sat calm and quiet, awed by the serenity she felt within. Then she broke the silence with hilarious laughter, and she laughed and laughed until she cried. For the first time in her life, peace and joy ruled over fear.

Understand that when Cari arrived for her next counseling session with me, I was unaware that any of this had happened. So at first glance, I was baffled. Before she said a word, I could see a difference in her countenance and demeanor. She seemed amazingly free of anxiety. The cloudy eyes I looked into before were now clear and bright. She seemed settled and carried herself more confidently. I knew I wasn't that good as a therapist. My curiosity was piqued.

Cari talked nonstop throughout our session, reviewing the details of what had happened since our last appointment and the difference God was making in her life. The voices were gone. She was sleeping through the night. She was experiencing inner peace like never before. When our forty-five minutes were up, she still had more to tell.

I had to chuckle at God's sense of humor. When Cari mentioned that the church she had visited was East Hill Church and that the pastor who helped her was named John, I knew immediately with whom she'd met. But she had no clue about this connection. I didn't say anything but smiled and thanked God for His gentle kindness. He knew of Cari's spiritual torment and orchestrated her encounter with people who could help. She thought she was on her way to collect garage sale treasures, but God had another treasure in store for her—a treasure far greater than the choicest diamonds and purest gold this world has to offer. The Spirit of God burst into Cari's darkness and flipped on the lights, he loosened her chains and sent them flying back to the pit. He gave a cowering young woman the ability to stand strong and tall with her head held high.

Several years have passed since I first met Cari. With great courage, she processed the many betrayals and abuses she suffered. One by one, she made the difficult but necessary choice to forgive her offenders. Cari doesn't believe that forgiveness means her offenders aren't responsible for their actions. Someday they will face God for their wrongs. But forgiveness purged the pain from Cari's heart and released her from a cancerous anger that would have eaten her alive. After she relinquished her bitterness to God, Cari's terrifying flashbacks disappeared. The memories remain, but they don't overpower her. The pain connected to the memories has been diluted. Now Cari says, "When the devil brings up my past, I just bring up his future."

As for the agoraphobia and panic attacks, they're gone, too. When you purge the pain, little remains to drive the panic. In fact, during the last couple of years, she has traveled abroad to share the Good News in Africa and in the former Soviet Union countries. Before, her anxiety drove her to avoid all travel. Now she's able to endure a twenty-two-hour plane ride without medication.

What's more, today Cari and her children are reconciled. To my amazement, she and her stepfather are on fairly good terms. It's rare that I witness any healing between an offender and a victim of incest. But in this case, that's how things turned out. Only God can enable that level of forgiveness.

Cari's transformation speaks volumes to me, and I've gleaned some lessons from her journey. I've learned that...

Some battles are clearly spiritual, not physical.

God will pull any captive out of the dark if he or she will stretch out a hand in faith.

When God intercepts a mom who is at the breaking point, He sends her home in her right mind.

If God will do it for Cari, He will do it for you and me. Hear the words of 2 Chronicles: "Do not be afraid or discouraged...for the battle is not yours, but God's....Stand firm and see the deliverance the LORD will give you" (20:15, 17). What battles will you let Him fight for you today?

Power Perk: A Taste of Hope

"Before we can be filled with the Spirit, the desire to be filled must be all-consuming. It must be for the time the biggest thing in the life, so acute, so intrusive as to crowd out everything else. The degree of fullness in any life accords perfectly with the intensity of true desire. We have as much of God as we actually want."

—A. W. Tozer[1]

"Great men are they who see that the spiritual is stronger than any material force."

—Ralph Waldo Emerson[2]

"Satan must be the most frustrated personality in the universe. His army of demons is compelled to obey Jesus, and whatever the devil does to discourage a Christian, God can use for the Christian's benefit."

—Billy Graham[3]

"I believe Satan to exist for two reasons: first, the Bible says so; and second, I've done business with him."

—Dwight L. Moody[4]

CHAPTER 17

When We Are Weak, He Is Strong

*M*y *grace is sufficient for you, for my power is made perfect in weakness."*

—2 Corinthians 12:9

The moment the little yellow bus pulled into our driveway, I knew the morning would to be a tearjerker. It was Nathan's first day of kindergarten and his first time to travel with a complete stranger. I was all tangled up inside. I knew Nathan's teacher, Stephanie Hadley, and I had every confidence Nathan would thrive in her class. But I also knew his vulnerabilities. Since he is handicapped, I feared the cruelties of others and how Nathan would sustain the harsh words that commonly fly from grade school mouths. If and when Nathan was mistreated, I wondered how we would ever know the full story, given his inability to talk.

Nathan wasn't aware of my hidden fears. With his Winnie-the-Pooh backpack tightly strapped on, he peered out the kitchen window, eager for his ride to arrive. When the bus finally came into view, Nathan produced a smile that would have melted the hardest of hearts. The entire family walked him out to the bus. I introduced him to the driver, and after formalities he gave me a half-dozen hugs, and said, "Bye, Mama." Then came multiple hugs for John, Jessie, Ben, and Kelli, a friend who lives with us. As the bus pulled out of the driveway and drove off, we blew kisses until we could no longer see each other. I went into the house, hid in the bathroom, and cried. Nathan had come so far to be able make this step.

Okay, I know I'm a softy. But I don't think I'm the only parent who has gone through a box of Kleenex in private.

Around noon it was me who was standing at the front window watching for the bus. When I saw it coming, it took me all of three seconds to make my way to the bottom of the driveway. Nathan saw me through the glass and frantically waved both hands, yelling, "Mama, Mama!" I had barely helped him off the bottom step of the bus when he started fishing through his backpack to show me his school papers. He was eager for me to know everything he had done. We went inside and reviewed the haphazard scribbles and lines on the papers. I noticed a sense of pride in Nathan I hadn't seen for a while. Come to think of it, he wore the same expression I saw him make one afternoon during a therapy session.

Shortly after Nathan was born, we enrolled him in an early intervention program, where multiple therapists exercised his mind and body to enhance his development. As an infant, Nathan's interventions were one-on-one, but toddlerhood moved him into a classroom setting with several special needs children. During the first part of class, the children met in a large open room where a physical therapist led them in group exercises to strengthen floppy muscle tone and work their gross motor skills. Upbeat music filled the room while the children made their best efforts to accomplish simple toe touches, arm reaches, hand claps, bends, and stretches.

I recalled watching similar routines when Jessie and Ben were in preschool. "Head, shoulder, knees and toes, knees and toes," the kids chimed along with the tape, keeping their motions in cadence with the music. Their movements jived with the beat. Their actions were precise, clearly defined, and consistent. But Nathan's class reflected a much different picture. The children's motions were awkward and rarely in sync with the leader's. If one of the children happened to dance in rhythm, it was usually more by accident than on purpose.

But there was a day when Nathan lit up with a sense of pride while delivering a perfect performance. He was in step with a therapist through the entire song. He didn't miss a beat. All his gestures were right on the mark. It wasn't because John and I had practiced with him umpteen times at home. It wasn't because his muscle tone had miraculously changed from floppy to firm.

Nevertheless, on this particular day, Nathan was selected for a demonstration. The therapist asked him to come to the front of the room and stand facing the class while she stood behind him.

"Nathan, lean back into me and put your hands in my hands," she instructed.

I watched Nathan relax his body into hers and place his little hands in her palms. When the music began, the therapist guided Nathan's arms through the routine. One, two, three, four. Up, down, all around. Together. Apart. Clap, clap, clap…

Nathan's droopy little arms did everything they were supposed to do as he let go and yielded to her lead. His assignment was to lean in and relax. The rest of the work was up to the therapist. Nathan's weakness was his greatest strength that day.

I embarrassed myself during that class. There we were in the middle of "up, down, clap, clap, clap," and I was wiping tears from my eyes. I secretly wondered if the other parents were thinking,

What's the big deal? She sure gets worked up over her son being picked to lead exercises!

But that had nothing to do with what was going on inside me. The Lord was talking to me through my son. He showed me my need to lean back and rest in the safety of my Father's arms. He nudged me to let go of the things that were troubling me.

With a keen awareness of my own handicaps, I sensed the Lord reassuring me that His grace would be sufficient for me. Should I lose my balance and stumble over bumps on this path called parenting, God will steady me and hold me up. When I get out of step, God will help get me back in sync. The greater my weakness, the greater God's strength.

Nathan has almost completed a year of kindergarten. Summer vacation is just around the corner. When the little yellow bus pulled into our driveway this morning, I fastened Nathan securely in his seat and gave him the usual five hugs and kisses before waving good-bye. Nine months have passed since we sent Nathan off to his first day of school. I haven't gone through a box of Kleenex in a while, but seeing his fragile hands waving wildly to me out the window still chokes me up now and then. Letting go doesn't happen without inner bleeding. But that's okay…I have someone behind me whose strength always holds me up when I'm weak. I don't have to be strong to be strong.

Power Perk: A Sip of Humor

A boy and his father traveled from their primitive area of the world to visit New York City. A cab driver suggested they stop and look around a shopping mall. They were amazed by almost everything they saw but especially by two shiny, silver doors that moved apart and back together again.

Looking inquisitively at the sliding doors, the boy asked, "What is this, Father?"

Since he had never before encountered an elevator, the father responded, "Son, I have never seen anything like this in my life. I don't know what it is."

While the boy and his father were watching in wide-eyed fascination, an older, white-haired lady with a cane hobbled up to the doors and pressed a button. The walls opened and the lady shuffled between them into the small room. The doors closed, and the boy and his father watched small circles of numbers above the walls light up. They continued to watch the circles light up in the reverse order. The walls opened up again and a beautiful twenty-four-year-old woman stepped out.

With wide-eyed wonder, the father immediately turned to his son and said, "Quick! Go get your mother!"

CHAPTER 18

Surprise Endings

*A*nd I will send showers, showers of blessings, which will come just when they are needed."

—Ezekiel 34:26, NLT

The touch of God on Marie cannot go unnoticed. It's in her eyes, her smile, her kindness, her patience. She is a prayer warrior with calloused knees and a tuned-in heart. I wouldn't say she walks on water, but as a mom, she comes close.

There were times when Marie wondered how she would survive the task of raising three children alone. How would she pay the bills? Get the kids to all their activities? Hold up under the strain of managing a job and a household without a partner? Through the years, those questions were answered by a faithful God who walked closely beside Marie during every step of her journey.

Marie wanted the best for her kids, just like every parent does. She was determined to be a devoted wife and attentive mother. She had every intention of blessing her children with a strong marriage, a safe home, and a family founded on love, acceptance, and forgiveness.

Unfortunately, life wasn't as neat and tidy as she had hoped. I'll let Marie tell her story....

* * * *

The rage and verbal abuse started early in our marriage. And when the children came along, the abuse escalated. We all walked on eggshells, wondering who would be the next to light Jay's fuse and bear his wrath. No matter how hard I tried, I couldn't change things. Most of what we did frustrated him. Minor inconveniences sent him into tirades. I suppose his affairs with other women were an attempt to escape the turmoil he felt inside. The infidelity went on for years, and our family bore the ugly scars of broken trust and betrayal.

I had considered leaving Jay before, but I avoided doing so because, more than anything else, I didn't want to disappoint God. I was raised to believe that divorce was just shy of an unpardonable sin. So I stayed, hoping and praying that things would get better. I confronted. I detached. I did everything I thought God wanted me to do…but nothing worked.

For years I tried hard to improve our marriage. I thought I was supposed to keep trying, no matter what. I thought it was righteous to give until it hurt. I thought I was being a good wife when I tried to stop Jay from doing harmful things. I wanted to support him in every way and help him get back on the straight and narrow path. I thought that was the Christian way.

Now I'm not so sure. The truth is, I couldn't control what Jay did, what he thought or felt, or how he chose to interact with me and our children, Jan, Jacque, and Jason. I could not control whether or not he chose to change his ways or get help for his sexual addiction. The more I tried to reason with him, the more defensive he became. I'm not exactly sure when the lights turned on, but at some point it became crystal clear that I needed to stop focusing on Jay. I needed to shift my focus back to managing my own life and meeting the children's needs.

Leaving Jay was the only viable option I could choose so the rest of us could survive. My health was at risk, and the children were suffering terrible blows to their self-esteem from his unpredictable rage and cruel barbs. The fears I had of becoming a divorce statistic paled in comparison to my fears of dying from a potential disease or of breaking under the strain of mental and emotional abuse. I made the hardest decision of my life and began looking for a place to live. For several weeks, I had searched for a three-bedroom apartment. Soon I received a phone call.

"Marie, I have good news and bad news for you."

The woman on the other end of the phone managed the apartment complex into which I was hoping to move. She said she had an apartment available, but only a two-bedroom. I wasn't in a position to be picky, but four people in a two-bedroom would be cramped! I prayed again and waited to see where God would lead us.

Jan and Jacque loved volleyball and wanted to attend a school with a strong athletic program. I presented this request to the Lord, knowing He would do what was best for the kids. I met with the Gresham School District's athletic director to see if the girls would be allowed to play volleyball if we relocated. Mr. Wolf assured me that they could play if they were good enough to make the team. Later that afternoon, I received a call from him.

"I talked to the Gresham High coach, and he definitely wants your girls to play volleyball," he said excitedly. Apparently the coach already knew of Jan's athletic abilities.

It sounded like divine direction, but we still hadn't found an apartment in the district. I mentioned to a mail carrier that I was looking for a place to live and wondered if he knew of any openings on his route. He called back that same day to say a three-bedroom apartment had just opened up that morning. It was a nice apartment in the Gresham School District, in an area Jan particularly liked.

Everything I specifically requested from the Lord was granted. Just one slight problem remained. The carpet in the new apartment was a horrible, greasy mess. The previous renter had worked on his motorcycle in the dining room, and huge oil stains permeated the entire floor. I asked the manager if the carpet was going to be replaced, and she said, "No, it will clean up nicely."

I gulped, convinced that no commercial solvent could strip that stuff. But I said to God, "If this is what you have chosen for us, then I will be thankful."

I can't say I would have responded as well in earlier years. Time and suffering had chiseled away my determination to demand my rights. Learning to trust God was the biggest challenge I had ever faced. But over and over, He proved to be faithful. His attentive love for me and my children was obvious in many tangible ways.

I recalled an incident from years before when I had asked God to provide piano lessons for the girls, even though we had no money for extras. Flo, a wonderful woman who lived on our street, just "happened" to be a piano teacher. Through our everyday comings and goings, Flo developed a friendship with my girls. One afternoon I heard a knock at my door. Flo was standing on the front porch wanting to know if I would let her teach the girls piano—free of charge! It was just something she thought would be fun to do. Flo became a dear friend and mentor to all of us, teaching us many lessons about life until the day she finished her fight with cancer and went home to be with the Lord.

Soon another call came from the apartment manager. "Marie, I've got good news and bad news."

I took a deep breath and thought, *Okay, God, I trust you.*

The manager continued, "The bad news is you can't move in on

Friday. We have to replace the carpet. The good news is you can move in on Saturday."

I hung up the phone and with a huge sigh of relief whispered, "Oh, God, you are so faithful!"

* * * *

Ten years had passed since Marie and her children moved into that little apartment. Like most families, they've had good times and bad times. But through it all, God was faithful. He taught them to push through their fears and view life as an adventure.

The girls went on to play volleyball for Gresham High School. Jan's team won the state championship two years in a row. Jacque's team won the championship the following two years. Marie spent many long nights and weekends watching practices and tournaments from gym bleachers. Little did any of them know the wonderful surprises God had in store for them.

Jan received a full scholarship to a university in Oregon, where she met the man of her dreams. They married and now minister to athletes in Colorado. On Sundays, you'll find Jan leading music during their church services.

Jacque also received a full scholarship—to a top Ivy League university, where she is now working on a master's degree. Her life is rich and fulfilling.

There is no possible way Marie could have provided these educational opportunities for her girls by herself. The resources simply weren't there. But God took care of His own.

The story wouldn't be complete without telling you about Marie's son. He wasn't as fortunate as the girls. The same opportunities didn't present themselves, and the family's problems left a deep wound that has yet to heal. But Marie has great faith that God is working on Jason in His own way. She recently told me something that came from her prayer time that rings with hope:

"I was troubled about Jason, and while I was praying, I said, 'God, it seems to me like you are here with me, and Jason is running as far as he can in the opposite direction.' That's when the Spirit said to me: 'It's okay, Marie. The earth is round.' I was shocked by the simplicity of His word and laughed out loud, declaring, 'Yes, God! The world is round, and Jason is going to come full circle and run right into you.'"

Marie hasn't seen the fulfillment of that word yet, but she believes with all of her heart that God will bring it to pass. To bolster her faith, she has tacked some verses in prominent places in her home. They are daily reminders of God's promises to her:

• "Where can Jason go from your Spirit? Where can he flee from your presence? If he goes up to the heavens, you are there; if he makes his bed in the depths, you are there" (Marie's paraphrase of Psalm 139:7–8).

• "I will contend with those who contend with you, and your children I will save" (Isaiah 49:25).

• "All your sons will be taught by the Lord, and great will be your children's peace" (Isaiah 54:13).

• "'As for me, this is my covenant with them,' says the LORD. 'My Spirit, who is on you, and my words that I have put in your mouth will not depart from your mouth, or from the mouths of your children, or from the mouths of their descendants from this time on and forever,' says the LORD" (Isaiah 59:21).

When others didn't keep their promises to Marie, God did. Marie had been a single mom for six years when the Lord brought a wonderful man into her life. God had to do some fancy maneuvering to place him in her path. When Marie's marriage to Jay ended, she knew that if she were ever going to have a relationship with another man, God would have to make the selection and bang her over the head to get her attention. As Marie put it, "My radar for good men was broken."

Well, God's wasn't. Darren is a man who has lovingly embraced Marie and her children. He unconditionally accepts and cherishes them in ways they never experienced before and frankly never dreamed possible.

I've heard it said that the definition of a righteous parent is not one who never falters or fails, but one who keeps getting back up. If life has knocked you flat, don't quit. Don't throw in the towel. Pick yourself up and keep charging ahead. Let go of what you can't control. Allow Marie's story to remind you that your needs, feelings, desires, and goals are extremely important to God. He cares what happens to your kids. When others fail you or your children, He won't! You may not be able to see it now, but God is working. Trust Him. Surprises await you, and they are likely better than you ever imagined.

So when unexpected dark clouds roll in and block out the light, remember that the forecast is for showers—showers of blessing. They're scheduled to arrive right on time, precisely when you and your children need them most.

Power Perk: A Taste of Hope

"You're blessed when you feel you've lost what is most dear to you. Only then can you be embraced by the One most dear to you."

—Matthew 5:3, *The Message*

—

"When it is a question of God's Almighty Spirit, never say, 'I can't.' "

—Oswald Chambers[1]

—

"When a train goes through a tunnel and it gets dark, you don't throw away your ticket and jump off. You sit still and trust the engineer."

—Corrie Ten Boom[2]

—

"Do good to your servant according to your word, O LORD."

—Psalm 119:65

—

"One is given strength to bear what happens to one, but not the one hundred and one different things that might happen."

—C. S. Lewis[3]

—

"May Jesus himself and God our Father, who reached out in love and surprised you with gifts of unending help and confidence, put a fresh heart in you, invigorate your work, enliven your speech."

—2 Thessalonians 2:16–17, *The Message*

CHAPTER 19

Lie Down in Your Soul

on't grieve God. Don't break his heart. His Holy Spirit, moving and breathing in you, is the most intimate part of your life....Don't take such a gift for granted."

—Ephesians 4:30, *The Message*

For eight years, I had the privilege of being mentored by Jean Lush. We were introduced by an editor, and we had fun writing two books together, *Mothers and Sons: Raising Boys to Be Men* and *Women and Stress: A Practical Approach to Managing Tension.* I hold those projects dear to my heart because as we wrote, Jean influenced me tremendously. I was in my thirties. She was in her seventies. We were both therapists with much in common, but her wisdom and life experiences far exceeded mine. Jean was a woman of deep faith, full of fascinating stories, and she had an intuitive sense about human nature. I'll always be grateful for the friendship we shared.

During one of my visits to Jean's English cottage, we sipped tea as she told about an experience she had when her daughter, Heather, was nine years old. At the time, Jean and her husband, Lyall, lived in a girls' dormitory at a private high school. Lyall taught classes, and Jean served as "dorm mother." One winter night, the principal of the school warned Jean to be on guard because he had heard a rumor that some girls were planning to sneak out of the dorm. Jean was on edge the whole evening, carefully watching for anything peculiar.

Around eight-thirty, Jean went to Heather's room to put her to bed. Their bedtime ritual was important to both of them, since it was hard for Jean to spend much one-on-one time with Heather during the day. Many girls in the dorm needed Jean's motherly encouragement and guidance, too.

On that night, Heather dawdled and delayed going to sleep. Jean was uptight and agitated because of the schemes she thought were being plotted behind her back. She was eager to get Heather in bed so she could go back to supervising the halls.

Jean tried to explain to Heather that she didn't have much time. But Heather ignored her, and Jean began to boil. Finally, Heather climbed into bed. Jean quickly covered her with blankets and stood, hoping to avoid further conversation. As Jean opened the door to leave, Heather said, "Mom, sit down on my bed and talk to me."

Jean sat on the edge of the bed, ready to jump up if she heard any suspicious sounds.

"Mommy, I want to talk to you," Heather said, growing more insistent.

"What is it, dear?" Jean replied.

"I can't talk to you when you're like this!"

Jean tried to relax and said, "Okay, dear, what do you want to say to me?" She was hoping there wasn't anything important to discuss.

"Please lie down with me," Heather said.

"Oh, all right."

Jean laid on the bed and waited for her daughter to say what was on her mind, but the little girl remained silent for a long time.

Finally, Jean said impatiently, "If you want to tell me something,

Heather, go ahead. Tell me about it now."

That's when Heather said something Jean never forgot.

"Mommy, I can't talk to you the way you are tonight. You must lie down in your soul first."

The words hit Jean like a two-by-four smack between the eyes. She decided her daughter was more important than the distractions. She took a deep breath, looked Heather in the eye, and offered her undivided attention. Heather obviously felt the difference. After Jean settled onto the pillow next to her, Heather unloaded a burden she had been carrying all day.

The kids in her class had teased her about her lisp. The teacher had made fun of her in front of the class by mimicking her and saying she spoke baby talk. Heather cried and cried and asked her mother why she hadn't told her she sounded so awful. Jean assured Heather that the problem would be handled the next day.

The following morning, Jean spoke to the principal, who specialized in helping children with speech problems. Heather began therapy right away, and in time the lisp was corrected.

Heather's words have stayed with me through the years. I try to remember to "lie down in my soul," particularly when I tuck in the kids at night. That's when all the events of the day catch up with them. The diversions have stopped, and they have time to think. To be honest, I wish the catch-up time didn't happen at night, since I'm usually exhausted. Sometimes all I want to do is get the kids through the bedtime routine so I can collapse for an hour before turning out the lights. Because I am a morning person, I've often wished their burdens could be laid down at 6:00 A.M. after I've had a piping hot espresso! No such luck. They're dead to the world at that hour.

One time, however, I woke up Jessie in the early morning for a heart-to-heart talk before school. I hadn't slept much the night before. She had shared some things with me at bedtime that troubled me. I left the conversation with a heavy heart. At the time, I mostly listened, unsure how best to respond.

I prayed through the night for wisdom and insight. Around five-thirty, I awoke again, replaying the conversation from the night before.

I said, "Lord, what should I do?"

I didn't hear an audible voice, but two words passed clearly through my mind: "There's more."

That was it. No solutions. No strategies. No formulas. Just "There's more."

Well, I thought, *I better find out what that means.*

I quietly crawled out from under the covers and fixed myself a cup of coffee. Whispering a prayer, I went in to wake up Jessie. With sleep still clouding her eyes, she sat up in bed and wondered what was going on.

Awkwardly, I said, "I know you don't like to get up this early, but when I was praying about what you shared with me last night, I believe I heard the Lord say to me, 'There's more.' Can you tell me what that means?"

I got a stunned gaze in response.

This was followed by a bucket of tears and the rest of the story. Some of the information was hard to hear, but it was absolutely critical for me to know so I could effectively handle the situation.

I will never forget the words God spoke to me during the wee hours of the morning. I was troubled, confused, and afraid. God knew that, and He guided me. Things were shared that may have not been disclosed had I not listened to Him and acted on His counsel.

I'm so thankful I didn't shrug off the words I heard or deny them in order to avoid conflict. It makes me all the more eager to listen to the Spirit as we continue on through uncharted territories. It makes me want never to take for granted the power of the One who intimately knows every detail about my children and me.

When the Holy Spirit gives direction and we respond, we will see results. Sometimes things may get worse before they get better. That's often how things work in this world. But in God's economy, pain always serves a purpose.

We cannot fool our kids or God about our attentiveness. So when we listen, let's lie down in our soul first. Our children will be more likely to get through to us. And the Holy Spirit will, too.

Power Perk: A Sip of Humor

This is a list of announcements that were printed in church bulletins …OOPS!

* Remember in prayer the many who are sick of our church and community.

* Thursday night—potluck supper. Prayer and medication to follow.

* For those of you who have children and don't know it, we have a nursery downstairs.

* The rosebud on the altar this morning is to announce the birth of David Alan Belzer, the sin of Mr. and Mrs. Belzer.

* This afternoon there will be a meeting in the south and north ends of the church. Children will be baptized on both ends.

* A bean supper will be held on Tuesday evening in the church hall. Music will follow.

* At the evening service tonight, the sermon topic will be, 'What is hell?' Come early and listen to our choir practice.[1]

CHAPTER 20

Troublemakers

ove your enemies and pray for those who persecute you."
—Matthew 5:44

When Ken was in the seventh grade, he had problems with a bully who humiliated him daily. He tripped Ken in class, yanked his chair out from underneath him, shoved his head in the water fountain when he was getting a drink, and made caustic remarks about him to others.

Ken's peace-loving personality tolerated this mistreatment for weeks until one day he finally reached his limit. Bursting into the house after an awful day at school, he poured out his heart to his mother, Nancy, detailing everything the bully had done since school began. Like any other conscientious mother, Nancy wanted to do whatever she could to help her son. Wrapping her arm around his shoulder she said,

"Ken, for some reason this kid has set himself up as your enemy," she said. "We don't know why, but I believe we can do something about it."

Ken's discouraged face lit up with hope as he waited to hear her idea.

"We need to say some serious prayers for this kid," Nancy continued. "God tells us to pray for our enemies. I believe if we do what God says, He will help you." From that day forward, they closed their evenings by praying for the "mean kid" in the class.

As the weeks passed, the mistreatment gradually dwindled. Within two months, the two boys were sitting together on the bus as field trip partners. School ended and Ken didn't see much of the troublemaker over the summer. But the following fall, the boy and his mother stopped by Ken's home to buy a jacket Ken had outgrown. The moms chatted over a cup of tea in the kitchen while the boys played. During their conversation, the other mother paused and with a twinkle of gratitude in her eyes told Nancy, "My son just thinks the world of Ken!"

Many years have passed since those nasty run-ins at school. Teachers and classes have come and gone. Several outgrown jackets hang in the back of both boys' closets. Ken never really understood why the bully chose to pick on him. But it doesn't matter. Today, the boys are in high school, and Ken's former bully is now his good friend. They may be as different as night and day, but that doesn't keep them from being pals. The other kids they spend time with don't understand their tight bond. Ken simply calls it a "God thing."

What started out a curse turned into a blessing. This former bully and his entire family visited the church Ken and Nancy attended and started a new and exciting relationship with God.

Now when Ken has a problem with a troublemaker, he comes home, vents his frustration, and then says, "Mom, he's just asking for it!"

Prayer, that is.

Power Perk: A Taste of Hope

"My troubles turned out all for the best—they forced me to learn from [God's] textbook."

—Psalm 119:71, *The Message*

"It doesn't matter how great the pressure is. What really matters is where the pressure lies—whether it comes between you and God or whether it presses you nearer His heart."

—Hudson Taylor[1]

"The world is full of so-called prayer warriors who are prayer-ignorant. They're full of formulas and programs and advice, peddling techniques for getting what you want from God. Don't fall for that nonsense. This is your Father you are dealing with, and he knows better than you what you need."

—Matthew 6:8, *The Message*

"Prayer does not change God, but changes him who prays."

—Soren Kierkegaard[2]

"This is the kind of life you've been invited into, the kind of life Christ lived. He suffered everything that came his way so you would know that it could be done, and also know how to do it, step by step."

—1 Peter 2:21, *The Message*

CHAPTER 21

House Call

*Y*ou cannot drink the cup of the Lord and the cup of demons too."
—1 Corinthians 10:21

Sometimes it's easy to get caught up in our day-to-day routines and forget that more is going on than our five senses can detect. A spiritual realm exists that is every bit as real as what we see, touch, taste, hear, and smell. Spirits are at war over our children, the most powerful being the Holy Spirit. His intention is always to bless, heal, restore, and help our children fulfill God's kingdom purposes.

However, dark spirits also have a mission to ensnare our children. They are crafty, evil, and deceptive. Satan, the great deceiver and author of lies, likes nothing more than to keep people oblivious to his strategies. As long as people believe that hell and evil spirits are just a bunch of mumbo jumbo, he has the upper hand.

John was scheduled as the pastor on call at the church during a typical day—typical, that is, until four-thirty in the afternoon when a call was transferred to his office. John picked up the receiver and heard the quavering voice of a frightened young man on the other end of the line.

"Uh, are you a minister?"

"Yes," John said. "Is there anything I can do to help you?"

"Yeah, I need someone to come to my house right away!" the young man said. "I'm here with my two friends and weird stuff keeps happening!"

"What do you mean by 'weird stuff'?"

"You aren't gonna believe me if I tell you."

"Well, give me a try," John said. "What's going on?"

"Pictures are dropping off the walls, and the TV keeps turning on and off by itself. There's something really bad going on in this house."

After writing down directions, John made a house call.

Three pale, skittish teenagers greeted him at the door. They were sixteen or seventeen years old and seemed like your average high schoolers. None of them went to church, but they had heard about East Hill from some other kids at school.

John sat with them on the living room couch and listened to their stories about the strange happenings. The boy who lived there hadn't been able to sleep at night because odd noises kept waking him up.

Curious to know how they perceived these bizarre occurrences, John asked, "What do you think is going on here?"

"I don't know, but it all started when we were playing with the Ouija board."

While John was talking with these young people, the television, which had been turned off, suddenly came on with the volume cranked up full blast. John saw the remote control sitting on the table in front of him and knew no one had touched it.

"See! See! That's what we mean!" one of the boys shouted. "Now you'll believe us!"

John investigated further. No other remote control devices were in the house, and no one else was home. The teens' stories were consistent, and the terror in their eyes was nothing shy of horrific. John knew something outside the natural realm was happening when the television didn't respond to him clicking off the power on the remote and the TV itself. He finally had to pull the plug from the wall to be able to continue his discussion with the kids.

John went on to explain to these young people that their Ouija board wasn't an innocent form of fun and games. It had likely opened a door to the dark powers that were harassing them.

"The Bible says that God is the only one who has power over dark forces," he told them. "If you have a relationship with Him, you don't have to put up with this kind of harassment."

"So what do we do?" one of the boys asked. "How do we get it?"

John answered, "You aren't going to get 'it'—you're going to get 'Him.' It's His power through you that will stop this stuff from happening."

The boys didn't want to waste another second. Right then and there, John led them in a simple prayer. All three of them said yes to God and no to the devil. They burned their Ouija board and decided they didn't want to open anymore doors to hell. Firsthand experience taught them a truth penned centuries ago by someone who kept company with Jesus: "Submit yourselves, then, to God. Resist the devil, and he will flee from you" (James 4:7).

Many young people unknowingly open the door of their lives to dark powers. As parents, we need to be wise to these schemes and teach our children to discern lies. If your son or daughter is experimenting with games, books, music, or anything else that might lead them into the evil one's grip, intervene! Put a stop to it. Point out where that path is heading.

As for the teenage boys, John hasn't received any more frantic calls. Hopefully, they learned once and for all to tap only into the source of life-giving power.

Power Perk: A Sip of Humor

Entertaining signs found around the country…

* On a maternity room door: Push! Push! Push!

* In a hospital: No Children Allowed in the Maternity Wards.

* On a residential fence: Salesmen welcome. Dog food is expensive.

* On a professional office complex: We shoot every third salesman, and the second one just left.

* In a Laundromat window: Ladies, leave your clothes here and spend the afternoon having a good time.

* On a veterinarian's door: Back in ten minutes. Sit. Stay.

* On an electrician's truck: Let us remove your shorts.

* On a funeral home: Drive carefully; we'll wait.

* On a residential front door: Everyone on the premises is a vegetarian except the dog.

CHAPTER 22

Parenting a Prodigal

I *will refine them like silver and test them like gold. They will call on my name and I will answer them; I will say, 'They are my people,' and they will say, 'The LORD is our God.'"*

—Zechariah 13:9

Years ago, when John and I first started teaching junior and senior highers, we met a striking young couple named Sharon and Kurt who volunteered to help. We had great admiration and respect for these two because of their wise parenting style and devotion to their children. You couldn't find more dedicated parents. They walked their talk and demonstrated love in action. Others viewed them as a model family and turned to them for counsel.

Somewhere along the way, we lost track of them. John and I transitioned out of youth ministry, and God led Sharon and Kurt to help begin a new church. We didn't see each other for many years. Their children grew up while we were giving birth to our three little ones. A while back, we ran into these old friends. The fifteen years we were apart left us all with a few more smile lines and gray hairs (only on the men), but once we started talking, it was just like old times. Eager to renew acquaintances, we set a time to get together and spent an afternoon visiting with Kurt and Sharon on the porch of their lovely home.

While sipping iced tea, we smiled over pictures of Jessie, Ben, and Nathan, and they proudly showed us snapshots of their sons, Jason and Matthew. That's when the story I want to share with you began to unfold. Many of the things they told us were deeply personal and best communicated firsthand. I've asked Sharon to tell their story.…

* * * *

The sound of emergency vehicles racing to Matthew's aid was more than my mind could comprehend. I held my son's head in my lap. His eyes were rolled back. His body shook with seizures. How did this happen? Only moments before, he had been riding his skateboard, laughing and joking with his friends. Now his baseball cap and skateboard lay crushed and scattered in the school parking lot. Sirens screamed. Lights flashed. Fire engines and police cars screeched to a halt near us. Paramedics ran full speed toward us and asked me to step aside while they assisted my son. My eyes scanned his thin frame. He looked so fragile.

I rode in the ambulance and watched intently as the paramedics worked to stabilize Matthew. I couldn't believe the messages I heard communicated to the hospital. Surely, it wasn't my son they were talking about: "Fifteen-year-old male, possible brain damage, pupils nonreactive, seizure activity, unconscious, deep bruising on the lower abdomen…"

A car had hit Matthew. He was thrown over the top of the vehicle and landed headfirst on the pavement. For thirteen days, he lay unconscious after sustaining severe injury to his brain. When Matthew awoke from the coma, he was not the same young man. He had turned extremely angry—angry with God, angry with his doctors, angry with his brother, angry with Kurt and me.

Through several months of physical therapy, his frustrations seemed to build. The accident left his motor skills and short-term memory impaired. Before the accident, Matthew was an honor student. Afterward, he could not retain simple information. His grades suffered and so did he.

When Matthew was sixteen, his anger and rebellion intensified. At seventeen, he left home. We didn't hear from him for several months or even know if he were alive. Kurt and I were traumatized. How could the little boy I had held in my arms for so many years reject our love?

Fear was my constant companion. Nighttime dreams were riddled with as much anxiety as my daytime thoughts. I had visions of receiving more bad news about Matthew. So many bad things had already happened to him that it was hard to defend against grave thoughts of something worse happening. I worried about his safety. I feared for his life.

I experienced heart palpitations and chest pains daily. My doctor said, "You have to let go of some stress." But how? I had no idea how to let go of my concerns for Matthew. He was my son, my flesh and blood.

Moments of relief came when I wrote in my journal. Every day I filled the pages of this little book with my deepest emotions. Some of the entries were prayers. Others were promises God whispered to me. Still others were letters to Matthew.

One afternoon when I was home alone, I had fallen asleep while reading a book. Something startled me, and when I awoke I felt as if I were drowning in waves of despair, unable to catch my breath. I cried out to God, and with perfect clarity, I heard Him say, "My daughter, I am here." The spirit of heaviness left me immediately.

Time and again, God rescued me from that sea of grief.

After months without news, we finally heard from Matthew. He called to tell us he was living with a friend and he wanted to see us. We were overjoyed, hoping this would be the beginning of reconciliation. But after that visit, we found ourselves more overwhelmed with sorrow than before. Matthew was still rebellious and angry.

I pondered the situation for days. Restless, confused, and unable to find peace, I found it impossible to sleep. My chest pains returned. Breathing was difficult. Once again, the struggle drove me to my knees and I surrendered Matthew back to God. While reading my Bible one afternoon, a passage in Isaiah helped to shift my focus:

> Do you not know? Have you not heard? The LORD is the everlasting God, the Creator of the ends of the earth. He will not grow tired or weary, and his understanding no one can fathom. He gives strength to the weary and increases the power of the weak. Even youths grow tired and weary, and young men stumble and fall; but those who hope in the LORD will renew their strength. They will soar on wings like eagles; they will run and not grow weary, they will walk and not be faint. (Isaiah 40:28–31)

The Spirit of God reminded me that though I was weary, God was not. Though I didn't understand a thing, God understood all. Though my young man, whom I loved so dearly, was stumbling and falling, God was stable and secure. And He would give me the strength I needed to keep going.

I recall saying to Kurt, "I will be so happy when Matthew comes back home." The comment was barely off my tongue when I sensed the Spirit saying to me, "Start celebrating now, before it happens."

The message was somewhat confusing, but the more I pondered His words, the more I realized what God was asking of me. He wanted me to demonstrate my faith. He wanted me to start living as if Matthew's return was in progress. I wanted to "see" before I believed, but God was saying, "If you believe, you will see." He wanted me to trust His power, His wisdom, and His timing. He wanted me to trust *Him.*

God was teaching our family a lesson during this time. He did not want us to wither and die while Matthew was away. Our oldest son, Jason, was the one who put the issue on the table. The three of us were in the kitchen talking when Jason said, "When will we ever laugh and be happy again? We have to find our joy again, even while we are waiting for Matthew to come back."

Jason was right. We had isolated ourselves because we didn't want to risk being hurt. We had stopped having people into our home. We feared being vulnerable and exposing our problems. We didn't have the stamina to deal with critical or judgmental attitudes.

I see now that the isolation fed our anguish. When we were alone, we were unable to draw strength from others. We didn't allow those who had been through similar trials to strengthen us. We had closed people out. I believe that is exactly where the enemy of our souls wanted us—withdrawn, alone, without hope.

I also realized that my spiritual life had become narrow and constricted. During my personal worship times, I inserted Matthew's name into Scripture verses and praise songs. One day when I was singing my prayers for Matthew, the Spirit of God challenged me, saying, "I have promised you that Matthew will come back to Me. Will you trust Me, even if you never see these promises fulfilled during your lifetime?" Then came a more important question: "My daughter, what has become of our relationship?"

It was a painful revelation. I realized how long it had been since I'd spent any time with God without making Matthew the center of our conversation. Somehow I had gotten trapped into thinking that the fervency of my prayers and songs would bring my prodigal home. In a sense, Matthew had become an idol, stealing my affections away from my heavenly Father. The realization grieved me, yet at the same time I felt such comfort from this reminder of God's jealous love for me.

One of the hardest days of my life occurred when we received a letter from our church, asking Matthew not to return. They didn't want him influencing others in a negative way. At the time, we had been in touch with Matthew mostly by phone. Now and then, he visited our home. Positive changes were happening in him. The letter from church caught us completely off guard. Those we thought would be our greatest support betrayed us. Bitterness began to take root.

Kurt and I knew we were in the midst of a refining fire. And we knew we had to make some hard choices. We could allow God to refine us, or we could give in to bitterness and allow the flames to consume us. God had seen the times we had judged others with prodigal children. Now we were the ones being judged. We were leaders in our church at the time, and we knew if we left in anger, many people would suffer. We stayed out of obedience to God, and He gave us the supernatural ability to do what we couldn't have done in our own power. We looked into the faces of those who were judging our parenting skills and chose to forgive them. In the process, God replaced our tendencies to judge with empathy for parents who, like us, were awaiting their prodigal's return. As we extended grace to others, God poured out His grace to us. The more we gave, the more we received. When our forgiveness was complete, God led us on to a safe place within another church body.

We tried our best to help Matthew in every possible way. When he called or visited, we gently suggested ways to help him improve the quality of his life. It seemed like the responsible thing to do. But it wasn't. One evening, Matthew came for dinner, and we enjoyed chicken and mashed potatoes along with lighthearted and casual conversation. The guys were talking about things they were looking forward to, and Kurt turned to Matthew and said, "If you ever want to go to college, we'll be happy to cover the tuition. The money is already set aside, if you ever want to use it."

Agitated, Matthew said, "What if I never change? What if this is all I ever turn out to be? Will you still love me?"

We saw that night the pain our "helpful hints" evoked in Matthew. The following day when Kurt and I were praying, God made it clear that our "guiding" responsibilities were over. All He wanted us to do now was love Matthew unconditionally. He told us that it would not be a person who would penetrate Matthew's defenses—it would be the Holy Spirit. We both heard him saying, "Through your love, I will reveal my love." It is hard to describe the freedom this gave us. The guidance, direction, leading, and teaching were now God's responsibility. All we had to do was love Matthew. That's it.

Matthew is now twenty-one, and Jason is twenty-four. Last Christmas I made photo albums for each of them, filled with snapshots from our camping and ski trips, our motor home expeditions across the United States, our adventures at Disneyland, and other special family memories. As Matthew flipped through the pages of his album, I watched a haze of sadness descend upon his face.

"Is there a problem, Matthew?" I asked gently.

"Mom, I know these pictures are of me, but I don't remember any of these times. I don't remember anything before my injury. I just remember waking up angry...angry at everything and everyone."

I was devastated. How could he not remember the wonderful family times? It was inconceivable to me that all the positive memories we so carefully created during his childhood had been washed away by the accident.

Fear gripped my soul. My head began to spin with questions. What if his spiritual foundations had vanished, too? What if all we taught him as a child had been erased? Once again, the Holy Spirit interrupted my anxiety with truth: "Sharon, God has known this all along."

Though this was new information to me, it was not new to God. Really, nothing had changed. The recall had been gone for years. I was assured that Matthew's memory loss did not nullify God's promises to me.

Since that incident around the Christmas tree, we have prayed daily for the healing of Matthew's memory. It is a slow process, but bits and pieces of the past are beginning to filter into the present. With each new memory, we see more of our son emerge.

It has been seven years since Matthew left home. Kurt and I have been on a journey that we would not wish on anyone. There has been much heartache along the way. But one truth stands tall above the rest: God's faithfulness echoes through time. Our prodigal is not "home" yet, but I know he is just around the bend.

How do we know? Because God has promised to bring Matthew home, and each new day takes us a step closer to that reality. As we have loved him without conditions, he has begun to heal. Matthew and his grandfather (my dad) are very close. Dad is now dying of cancer, and Matthew prays for him every day. God can use anything to accomplish His purposes.

Matthew has also developed a close friendship with his brother and new sister-in-law. He calls Kurt and me daily to say, "I love you, Mom and Dad." We have come a long way in seven years. Our angry young boy, who once lived on the streets, is now a loving son who welcomes us into his life. I am so glad we did not wait to see Matthew coming around the bend before we thanked God for His faithfulness. So much joy would have been lost through the years.

I'd like to leave you with some final thoughts. One of the biggest lessons Kurt and I have learned is that Satan is an accuser who works overtime to steal joy and heap on condemnation. He knows when we are weak and capitalizes on our vulnerabilities. We have learned to recognize his sinister taunts and replace his lies with God's truth.

He cackles and mocks us, saying, "Matthew is lost!" But we argue, "He who began a good work in Matthew will see it through to completion." When dark forces rail against us with the lie "God has forsaken you," we fight back with, "God says He will never leave us or forsake us."

Oh, friend, don't believe the lies Satan tells you. Hear the Spirit whisper fresh promises from the heart of the Father: "Don't give up. Don't quit. Trust Me. Surrender that which you hold dear to your heart. Come into my everlasting arms and let me hold you. Take my hand. I will lead you through the dark and turn your mourning into joy. I will be faithful to you and to your children. The world says you must see to believe. I say to you, 'If you believe, you will see.'"

* * * *

Postscript: Recently, Kurt and Sharon received a call from Matthew asking if he could move home. They are now unpacking boxes and beginning a new chapter in their lives. Their prodigal is home, and they have declared this as their Year of Jubilee.

Power Perk: A TASTE OF HOPE

"Jesus did not come to explain away suffering or remove it. He came to fill it with His presence."

—Paul Claudel[1]

"Fear not, for I am with you. Do not be dismayed. I am your God. I will strengthen you; I will help you; I will uphold you with my victorious right hand. I am holding you by your right hand—I, the Lord your God—and I say to you, Don't be afraid; I am here to help you."

—Isaiah 41:10, 13, TLB

"To be able to explain suffering is the clearest indication of never having suffered."

—Oswald Chambers[2]

"How can you say that the Lord doesn't see your troubles and isn't being fair? Don't you yet understand? Don't you know by now that the everlasting God, the Creator of the farthest parts of the earth, never grows faint or weary? No one can fathom the depths of his understanding. He gives power to the tired and worn out, and strength to the weak. Even the youths shall be exhausted, and the young men will all give up. But they that wait upon the Lord shall renew their strength. They shall mount up with wings like eagles; they shall run and not be weary; they shall walk and not faint."

—Isaiah 40:27–31, TLB

CHAPTER 23

Critics

*D*on't pick on people, jump on their failures, criticize their faults—
unless, of course, you want the same treatment."

—Matthew 7:1, *The Message*

"It's been a truly awful week," Laura said as she settled into the chair across from me. "I feel like I've been ambushed."

I could tell from the strain on her face that this mother of four was trying to hang on for dear life. The winds of adversity had stormed across her soul like a hurricane. She had more chronic stresses than the average mom—a son with a severe case of Attention Deficit Disorder, a teenage daughter who suffered from depression, and two preschoolers who ran circles around her from sunup to sundown. But on the day she came to see me, those issues took a backseat to a more pressing problem—a problem familiar to most of us who have children.

As Laura replayed the events of the week, I could see she had endured the painful blows of a critic. Another parent from school had assumed the role of judge and jury and pronounced her daughter, Mandy, a "problem kid." The woman viewed Mandy as a bad influence on others in the class. Laura learned that this woman had felt it her "duty" (presumption) to "inform" (gossip with) several other parents about Mandy.

Wiping tears from her eyes, Laura told me, "My friend called me yesterday and asked if I knew what was being said about Mandy. I didn't have a clue. She told me that she and several other parents had been 'warned' about Mandy by another mother. My friend has known Mandy for years and was troubled by what she heard. Out of loyalty, she called me."

Few things carry a blistering sting like misdirected judgment and criticism. Most of us have experienced it—the gut feeling that someone sees us as unacceptable. They think we are either "too this" or "too that." Being on the receiving end of a fault-finding eye can suck the life out of even the heartiest of souls. It's even worse when that criticism is aimed at our children.

For a few moments, Laura and I explored the feelings this series of events tapped into. She was angry someone had pigeon-holed her daughter. She was embarrassed her family was being cast in a negative light. But Laura's fuse was lit when she learned this critic also had slammed her ability as a mom, saying she should quit her part-time job at the bank and make her kids more of a priority. That one pushed major guilt buttons! What's more, Laura feared that others would believe the critic and ostracize her daughter.

I knew Mandy casually. She seemed to be a typical ninth-grader, who struggled with mood swings and self-esteem. But she had friends, did fine in school, and even volunteered as a candy striper at the local hospital. From my recollections, I couldn't think of anything that would lead people to believe she was a "problem." I wondered what motivated the gossip.

Come to find out, Mandy and the critic's daughter, Patty, had been buddies since the third grade. They went to school together, played sports, and shared many of the same friends. But things changed when the girls started ninth grade. Mandy made the varsity basketball team. Patty didn't. Patty's mother thought the decision was political. Enter jealousy.

Shortly thereafter, Mandy and Patty got into a tiff over usual adolescent stuff and exchanged sharp words. Patty told her mom what happened, which launched the campaign to "fix" Mandy— behind her back, passive-aggressively. Rather than encouraging Patty to talk things through with Mandy, this angry mom made it her mission to inform the world that Mandy was a "bad" girl and that her daughter Patty had been an innocent victim. Naturally, the mother never mentioned Patty's contribution to the conflict.

Laura and I agreed that this was not going to be the last time someone criticized her or her children. Critics lurk around every bend in the road. She wanted to develop a strategy to deal with these situations in a way that facilitated healing and growth. After all, what we model to our children in response to these situations has far more power in their lives than the situations themselves.

I shared with Laura what a wise woman—eighty-two years young—once told me. She said, "Pam, your job is not to raise godly children."

Her comment hit me between the eyes. I crinkled my nose and said, "What? You better run that by me again."

"Your job is not to raise godly children," she repeated. Then she added, "Your job is to be a godly role model for your kids. God has given them a free will, and He is the one who will ultimately have the greatest shaping power in their lives. Your job is simply to do your part by modeling godly behavior."

I, too, have been in Laura's position and suffered the pain of watching my children say unkind things and make mistakes while growing up. What parent hasn't? I also have been on the receiving end of judgmental attitudes and felt the pain of having a child "categorized" in a less than positive light.

After Nathan was born with Down Syndrome, a lady approached me at church and said, "I'm praying that God will heal your son...." It started out nice, but then she added, "...because I don't believe God wants mongoloids running around on this earth." I was so stunned that all I could do was turn on my heels and walk away. It was probably best. Had I stayed, I might have punched her lights out.

I think it was Oswald Chambers who once said, "True spirituality is seen in the face of meanness."

Laura and I brainstormed ways she could turn this difficult situation into a lesson for Mandy. She decided to talk with her daughter about being kind to Patty and her mother, without looking for a payoff. Laura knew their perception of Mandy might not change, but that wasn't the point. God wanted Mandy and Laura to do what was right regardless of the results. They read 1 Corinthians 13 together and discussed how God's definition of love applied to their circumstance.

When I saw Laura a few weeks later, I learned that things had pretty well blown over at school. Patty and Mandy were on good terms again. And the critic? Well, the saga continues. Word has it she has "warned" a few more people about Mandy. Old gossip has been replaced with something new and juicier. That's the nature of wily words. But life goes on, and the worst of what Laura feared—that her daughter would be alienated—hasn't come to pass. By the way, it rarely does. Most everyone outlives criticism.

Hearing their story made me think back to my own childhood, recalling the people who had a significant influence on me. I thought of the ones who pulled the best out of me, those who accepted me as

I was, warts and all. That doesn't mean they didn't correct me when I did wrong. Believe me, I had my fair share of discipline. But I knew they didn't assume the worst possible motives behind my behavior. They looked beyond my faults and saw potential I didn't even know was present. They forgave my weaknesses and encouraged me to be the best I could be.

Children are works in progress. Life brings many situations their way to teach them. Mistakes are part of growing up. Since our children are in process, all judgments are provisional. Their story isn't over yet. They are constantly growing, being challenged beyond their current weaknesses and limitations.

It occurs to me that it really isn't fair to judge something until it is finished. And then it's probably best to leave that job to the One who canceled all judgments held against us, once and for all, at the cross.

Power Perk: A Sip of Humor

"The Lord made Adam from the dust of the earth, but when the first toddler came along, He added electricity."[1]

―――

"[Our son] William daily reenacts the feeding of the five thousand. We give him one small rice cake, and when he is finished, we clean up twelve baskets full of the remnants."

—Kenneth Draper[2]

―――

A letter from a college student to her parents…

Dear Mom and Dad,

I am sorry that I have not written, but all my stationery was destroyed when the dorm burned down. I am now out of the hospital, and the doctor said that I will fully recover. I also moved in with a boy who rescued me since most of my things were destroyed in the fire. Oh yes, I know that you have always wanted a grandchild, so you will be pleased to know that I am pregnant, and you will have one soon.

Love, Mary

P.S. There was no fire. My health is perfectly fine, and I am not pregnant. In fact, I do not even have a boyfriend. However, I did get a D in French and a C in math and chemistry. I just wanted to make sure you kept it all in perspective.[3]

CHAPTER 24

Hello, Bobby!

f or God so loved the world that he gave his one and only Son, that whoever believes in him shall not perish but have eternal life."
—John 3:16

In the early 1900s, a young woman named Mildred graduated from Kent State University and began teaching in a one-room schoolhouse. She was the first in her family of eleven children to complete a college education. A problem arose when she met the love of her life, because back then, women weren't permitted to teach after they married. The courtship lasted three years. Shortly after she was awarded her Lifetime Teaching Certificate, she married Claude Williamson against her family's wishes.

Established in their Ohio community, the couple decided to start a family. Tragically, their first two babies died in the womb. But after years of dreaming and praying, Charlene was born, and then their son, Bobby. Mildred stayed home with the children while Dad Williamson worked long hours earning their income. And Sunday? Well, it was the Lord's day, and the four of them joined the rest of the townsfolk at church, followed by a finger-licking, all-you-can-eat potluck.

One Sunday evening, after a long day of church activities, the family arrived home. Mildred felt unusually tired but figured it was nothing a good night's sleep wouldn't cure. Nine hours of slumber, however, did nothing to help her feel better. In fact, she woke up in the morning so sick with the flu she couldn't get out of bed. In those days, friends dropped in regularly to check on one another or to sip a glass of iced tea on the porch swing. Sure enough, a next-door neighbor stopped to visit and found Mildred weak and woozy. She offered to watch the kids for the day. With a sigh of relief, Mildred sunk deep into her feather bed and drifted off to sleep. It was a welcome escape from the blistering heat of the day and the misery of a stubborn, unbreakable fever.

Little Bobby and Charlene, the best of pals, were used to running from house to house while playing with children in their neighborhood. Since most moms were home during the day at that time, there was a community understanding that everyone kept an eye out for all the neighborhood kids as they congregated in one yard or another.

On this morning, however, two-year-old Bobby escaped the attention of all watchful eyes when he wandered over to the yard next door. Heavy rains had fallen that month in Ohio, and what looked like a shallow puddle turned out to be a four-foot-deep hole filled with rainwater. Bobby didn't know any better and plunged in, without the coordination or strength to pull himself out. Within minutes, he drowned.

A false report circulated around town that a severely handicapped boy had drowned. A drowning is always tragic, but somehow the townsfolk thought the incident was a "blessing in disguise." Some people said things such as, "Better the handicapped child be in heaven than suffer in this world."

But the truth soon emerged—the handicapped child was safe at home with his family. It was Bobby Williamson who had died.

Eventually Mildred recovered from the flu, but the grief over losing her little boy lingered for years. It was bad enough to lose two babies she had never had the chance to cuddle in soft, fluffy blankets. But this…this was unbearable.

Mildred and Claude tried to make the best of things as they went on with their lives. In time, the sadness they saw in their daughter's eyes over losing her best friend moved them to try again for another child. They conceived. But after what seemed to be a completely normal pregnancy, the baby was stillborn.

They struggled with the nagging thoughts most parents would entertain, given the same lot in life: *What did I do to deserve this? Why would God allow four children from a loving home to die?* Shortly after the baby's burial, Mildred concluded that she and God were no longer on speaking terms.

Before long, a call came from the local school superintendent. He had heard that Mrs. Williamson was a teacher before Charlene and Bobby were born, and he wanted her to come to work for him. She turned down the offer, thinking she couldn't face a classroom of children with her heart so full of grief. But the superintendent, relentless in his pursuit, was determined to fill the assignment with a top-quality teacher. After being prodded, coaxed, and cajoled, Mildred gave in and accepted the job offer.

Over the years, Charlene and the school children helped assuage Mildred's emotional pain. She could spend little time absorbed in her anguish when so many little ones needed her attention. She and her husband never were able to bring more children into the world, but for many years, she loved and cared for hundreds of children who were forever changed by her love.

Years later, when Charlene was in college, Mildred opened a private kindergarten that was attended by the children of those who worked in the nation's space program in Florida. This was before the public schools offered their own kindergarten programs. Many of those children grew up and brought their own children back to meet their "most favorite teacher of all."

I spent some time with Mildred Williamson a month short of her ninetieth birthday. She, my Aunt Charlene, Uncle Jim, and cousins had gathered for a weekend of family fun. Gramma Williamson was full of laughter, as sharp as a tack, and still deeply in love with children. I watched this elderly woman sit peacefully on the living room couch, while our little Nathan, then four years old, climbed all over her like a jungle gym and launched sprawling belly flops into her lap. Nothing ruffled her. Not the noise. Not the activity. Not the interruptions in the conversations. Not the other eight great-grandchildren scrambling for the seat next to her on the couch. And there were plenty of hugs and lap time for all interested parties.

Gramma Williamson never did understand why she wasn't given the chance to raise little Bobby. But somewhere along the line, she and God got back on speaking terms. She told me she no longer questioned God's love. That issue was settled for her when she realized her heavenly Father had also lost His one and only Son—for her sake.

Last Fourth of July, we celebrated a big family reunion back east. It wasn't quite the same. Gramma Williamson couldn't come this time. She was completing her final days in this world. Aunt Charlene and Uncle Jim stayed at her bedside around the clock. One evening, Jim sat with Gramma, studying her face and reflecting on the many experiences they shared together through the years. Gramma had been unresponsive for hours, wavering somewhere between this life and the next. Much to Jim's astonishment, she broke the silence with a tender smile and softly said, "Hello, Bobby." She then told Charlene and Jim of flowers and music that were unlike anything else she had ever seen or heard. A few hours later, Gramma and Grandpa Williamson, little Bobby, and their three other children had a wonderful family reunion in heaven.

Gramma Williamson was an interesting paradox. All who knew her said her uncanny wit made them laugh until their sides ached. And yet she suffered unimaginable pain during the nine decades she spent on earth. Two miscarriages. A stillbirth. The death of her two-year-old son. Add to this the fact that she survived the loss of all ten of her brothers and sisters. That's a lot of funerals for one woman! But somehow she was able to maintain her sense of humor. Much of her poetry reflected her whimsical sense of humor. This little jingle was found in the back of her well-worn Bible after she died.

DON'T WAIT TIL I'M GONE
When I quit this mortal chore
And mosey around this earth no more
Don't weep. Don't sigh. Don't sob.
I've likely struck a better job.
Don't go and buy a large bouquet
For which you'll find it hard to pay.
Don't mope around and feel all blue
I'm likely better off than you.
Don't tell the folks I'm a saint
Or any old thing I ain't.
If you have jam like that to spread,
Please hand it out before I'm dead.
　　　　　—Mildred Williamson

Gramma lived what she preached. She was the kind of person who left you feeling good about yourself and hopeful about the future. One of the things the three generations of family surrounding her often heard her say was, "Nothing will happen today that the Lord and I can't handle together." Oh, how I hunger for that level of confident trust in God as John and I and the kids navigate the rough waters of life.

Gramma knew she was on her way home. Shortly before she died, she penned a letter to her loved ones:

> My dear family and friends,
>
> The time has come for me to leave this world and go to a new home that has been prepared for me by our dear Lord. I have seen it only through my mind's eye and our most sacred of all books—our Bible. Surely, you must know that I am anxious to see what I have long wondered and dreamed about. It will surpass anything I have seen on this earth, I am sure.
>
> Now it is natural that I will be missed by some of you for a while. Make it just a little while, then place me in your book of memories with many lovely thoughts of the beautiful times we enjoyed together. Time, at best, is short and there is so much work to be done before you, too, will be called to your new home to be with all of us who have preceded you there. What a gathering that will be!
>
> May our dear Lord bless you in every effort you make to accomplish His purpose for you on this earth. I leave you now, with deep love and a happy heart. God bless you and keep you.
>
> Mildred Williamson

When my days on earth are complete, I know Gramma will be there to welcome me home with love and hugs and plenty of laughter. No doubt she'll be full of stories about her awesome adventures in heaven—and about the One who answered all the questions she had in this world. I've got some questions and stories tucked away for Gramma, too. It's a good thing eternity is forever. I have a feeling the stories and laughs will go on and on and on....

Power Perk: A Taste of Hope

"The Spirit can make life. Sheer muscle and willpower don't make anything happen. Every word I've spoken to you is a Spirit-word, and so it is life-making."

—John 6:63, *The Message*

"Those who follow after the Holy Spirit find themselves doing those things that please God. Following after the Holy Spirit leads to life and peace."

—Romans 8:5–6, TLB

"Prayer does not mean that I am to bring God down to my thoughts and my purposes, and bend His government according to my foolish, silly, and sometimes sinful notions. Prayer means that I am to be raised up into feeling, into union and design with Him; that I am to enter into His counsel and carry out His purpose fully."

—Dwight L. Moody[1]

Mother Teresa was once asked, "How do you love the unlovely?" She answered, "First, we meditate on Jesus, and then we go out and look for Him in disguise." Somewhere underneath our children's fussing and fuming, scrapping and squabbling, complaining and carrying on, is Jesus. Will you look for Him today?

CHAPTER 25

Restaurant Prayers

He answered their prayers, because they trusted in him."
—1 Chronicles 5:20

Our family loves to eat at El Ranchito's, a family owned Mexican restaurant near our home. Thankfully, going out for dinner is easier now than it used to be. Nathan now sits somewhat peacefully through a meal, but there was a time when he liked to play Houdini and slither out of his high chair (with two safety straps) to hide under the table. To him, it was a game. To us, it was mortifying, particularly when he would yell "Mama! Dada!" at the top of his lungs from around our feet. We figured he saw the dark crawl space as a spiffy fort and wanted us to come play. For some reason, he couldn't grasp the concept that we had to maintain a more refined public "image." Eating chips and salsa under the table wasn't okay for Mom and Dad or for him. So much for image management.

Funny things happen in restaurants. Kim told me about her six-year-old son who asked if he could say the prayer when the meal arrived. Everyone bowed their heads as he recited the following: "God is good. God is great. Thank you for the food, and God, I will even thank you more if Mom gets us ice cream for dessert, with liberty and justice for all! Amen!"

Along with the laughter from the other customers nearby, the little boy and his mom heard a rather uptight woman remark, "That's what's wrong with this country. Kids today don't even know how to pray. Asking God for ice cream! Why, I never!"

The little boy burst into tears and asked his mom, "Did I do it wrong? Is God mad at me?"

His mom gave him a big hug and assured him that he had done a terrific job and that God was not mad at him.

As she was consoling her son, an elderly gentleman approached their table. He winked at the youngster and said, "I happen to know that God thought that was a great prayer."

"Really?" the little boy asked.

"Cross my heart," came the reply. Then in a theatrical whisper, he added with a nod toward the woman whose remark had started the whole thing, "Too bad she never asks God for ice cream. A little ice cream is sometimes good for the soul."

Naturally, the boy was given a dish of ice cream at the end of his meal. When the waitress set it on the table, he stared at it for a moment, and then did something that startled his family. He picked up his sundae and without a word walked over and placed it in front of the stern woman.

With a big smile he said, "Here, this is for you. Ice cream is good for the soul, and my soul is good already."[1]

The next time your children express their faith in a way you think isn't quite "right," avoid the temptation to show them how it should be done. As long as they honor God and show Him respect, let them approach their Father any way they find natural and comfortable. Jesus said it succinctly: "Let the little children come to me, and do not hinder them, for the kingdom of God belongs to such as these" (Mark 10:14).

Power Perk: A Sip of Humor

A woman answered her front door and found two boys holding a list.

"Lady," one of them said, "we are on a treasure hunt, and we need three grains of wheat, a pork chop bone, and a piece of used carbon paper to earn a dollar."

"Wow," the woman replied, "who sent you on such a challenging hunt?"

"Our baby-sitter's boyfriend."[1]

One night, a teenage girl brought her new boyfriend home to meet her parents. They were appalled by his appearance: leather jacket, motorcycle boots, tattoos, and a pierced nose. Later, the parents pulled their daughter aside and confessed their concern.

"Dear," said the mother diplomatically, "he doesn't seem very nice."

"Mom," replied the daughter, "if he wasn't nice, why would he be doing five thousand hours of community service?"[2]

The best way to keep teenagers at home is to create a loving atmosphere—and then let the air out of their tires.

CHAPTER 26

Letting Go of Second Best

*I*f your first concern is to look after yourself, you'll never find yourself. But if you forget about yourself and look to me, you'll find both
yourself and me."

— Matthew 10:39, *The Message*

A cheerful girl with bouncy golden curls, Jenny was almost five.
Waiting with her mother at the checkout stand, she saw them: a
circle of glistening white pearls in a pink foil box.

"Oh, please, Mommy. Can I have them? Please, Mommy,
please!"

Quickly, the mother checked the back of the little box, and then
looked back into the pleading blue eyes of her little girl's upturned
face.

"It costs $1.95," she said. "That's almost two dollars. If you
really want them, I'll think of some extra chores for you, and in no
time you can save enough money to buy them for yourself. Your
birthday's only a week away, and you might get another crisp dollar
bill from Grandma."

As soon as Jenny got home, she emptied her piggy bank and
counted out seventeen pennies. After dinner, she did more than her

share of chores, and she went to ask their neighbor, Mrs. McJames, if she could pick dandelions for ten cents. On her birthday, Grandma did give her another new dollar bill. At last, Jenny had enough money to buy the necklace.

Jenny loved her pearls. They made her feel grown up and special. She wore them everywhere—Sunday school, kindergarten, even to bed. The only time she took them off was when she went swimming or had a bubble bath. Mother said if they got wet, they might turn her neck green.

Jenny had a loving daddy, and every night when she was ready for bed, he would stop whatever he was doing and come upstairs to read her a story. One night when he finished the story, he asked Jenny, "Do you love me?"

"Oh yes, Daddy. You know that I love you."

"Then give me your pearls."

"Oh, Daddy, not my pearls. But you can have Princess, the white horse from my collection, the one with the pink tail. Remember, Daddy? The one you gave me. She's my favorite."

"That's okay, Honey. Daddy loves you. Good night." And he brushed her cheek with a kiss.

About a week later, after story time, Jenny's daddy asked again, "Do you love me?"

"Daddy, you know I love you."

"Then give me your pearls."

"Oh, Daddy, not my pearls. But you can have my baby doll. The brand-new one I got for my birthday. She is so beautiful, and you can have the yellow blanket that matches her sleeper."

"That's okay. Sleep well. God bless you, little one. Daddy loves you." And as always, he brushed her cheek with a gentle kiss.

A few nights later when her daddy came in, Jenny was sitting on her bed with her legs crossed Indian-style. As he came close, he noticed her chin was trembling and a tear rolled down her cheek.

"What is it, Jenny? What's the matter?"

Jenny didn't say anything but lifted her little hand up to her daddy. And when she opened it, there was her little pearl necklace. With a little quiver, she finally said, "Here, Daddy. It's for you."

With tears gathering in his own eyes, Jenny's kind daddy reached out with one hand to take the dime-store necklace, and with the other hand he reached into his pocket and pulled out a blue velvet case with a strand of genuine pearls and gave them to Jenny. He'd had them all the time. He was just waiting for her to give up the dime-store stuff so he could give her genuine treasure.

So like our heavenly Father.[1]

Have you placed your life in His hands yet today?

Power Perk: A Taste of Hope

"The biggest blessing in your life was when you came to the end of trying to be a Christian, the end of reliance on natural devotion, and were willing to come as a pauper and receive the Holy Spirit."

—Oswald Chambers[1]

———

"The Lord doesn't want first place in my life. He wants all of my life."

———

"For where your treasure is, there your heart will be also."

—Matthew 6:21

———

"In the kingdom of God the surest way to lose something is to try to protect it, and the best way to keep it is to let it go."

—A. W. Tozer[2]

———

"Treasures in heaven are laid up only as treasures on earth are laid down."

CHAPTER 27

Church Camp

*H*e who belongs to God hears what God says."

—John 8:47

Jessie sat on top, and I pushed with all my might to close the latches on the old Samsonite suitcase. Somehow this rugged piece of luggage had survived twenty long years of wear and tear. I'd taken it on several trips abroad and who knows how many trips within the States to visit family. Now it was Jessie's for a week at church camp. She much preferred a brand-new Nike duffel bag, but Mom and Dad said "no go." Being former youth camp directors, we were all too familiar with how teens treated things in the cabins.

Later, as we waved good-bye to the buses, John turned to me and said, "I hope you know she's going to need a year of therapy when she gets home."

"Why is that?" I asked.

"Because of the abuse she's going to suffer from the others over that decrepit old suitcase!" he replied.

We laughed and figured our strong-willed firstborn would hold her own if anyone taunted her.

A variety of emotions surfaced as I watched the bus pull out of the parking lot. I felt excited that Jessie had the chance to learn more about God from great youth leaders. I felt hopeful that she would develop new friendships. I felt concern about her safety. (The downside of being a therapist is hearing the horror stories about children killed in accidents.) And frankly, I felt relieved that we were not the camp directors this time. It was someone else's turn.

We prayed for Jessie that week and asked God to speak to her. We invited Him to do whatever He wanted to do at this juncture of her journey. She was headed into the seventh grade in the fall, and we were eager for God to prepare her for the predictable adolescent storms ahead.

A week later, Jessie dragged herself off the bus, looking about as worn-out as her old blue suitcase. She was moving at a turtle's pace and appearing a bit glassy-eyed through all the smiles.

Come to find out, her cabin had pulled an all-nighter to stretch the camp experience. She had been up forty-eight straight hours. I felt sorry for the poor counselor who undoubtedly went home blurry-eyed and semiconscious. All I could think was, *I'm sure glad it wasn't me in that cabin at 4:00 A.M. with twelve giddy girls hanging from the rafters!*

"So how was camp?" I asked Jessie.

"Great!" she said.

"Did you have fun?"

"Yeah, it was a blast!"

"Did you make some neat friends?"

"Tons!"

"What kinds of things did God teach you?"

"Oh, I don't know. I'm too tired to talk about it now."

"Okay."

It took all of us a few days to regain our equilibrium after the re-entry into real life. Hormonal teenagers and all-nighters are a lethal combination. But while we were sitting around the dinner table one evening, Jessie shared a story that we will always hold dear.

"God spoke to me when I was at camp," she announced.

"Really?" I replied, doing my best to monitor any overreaction. "When?"

"It was one night during chapel when we were singing worship songs," she said matter-of-factly. "God spoke to a lot of kids that night."

"What did He say to you?" John asked.

"He told me He didn't want me to be an ophthalmologist."

I admit, I hadn't expected to hear that. I'm not sure what I expected. Perhaps I had some secret hopes that she would say something like, "God told me never to argue with my mom and dad, to keep my room clean, and to do all my chores without ever complaining again." No such luck. Oh, well.

Jessie had my undivided attention because I knew how determined she was to become a doctor. She had seriously entertained this goal for several years. She had written reports about it and interviewed health care professionals for school assignments. I was curious to know more.

"Jessie, why do you think God told you that?"

"I don't know, Mom," she said. "But I know the thoughts didn't come from me because I've wanted to be an ophthalmologist for a long time."

"Did God give you any other direction?"

"Nope. But whatever He wants will be good."

I smiled, agreed, and marveled at the deep work God had done in this young teen in just six days. Jessie had heard the Spirit of God speak to her—clearly and specifically. And she had confidence that

God's plans for her future were good. She was way ahead of me when I was that age.

It was the beginning of an answer to many prayers John and I had spoken since the kids were infants. We wanted them to be able to hear the Spirit speak to them at an early age. We had read stories in Scripture, such as the one featuring Samuel, the little boy whom God woke up in the wee hours of the morning for a heart-to-heart conversation about future events. You remember the story....

> Little Samuel was helping the Lord by assisting Eli. Messages from the Lord were very rare in those days, but one night after Eli had gone to bed (he was almost blind with age by now), and Samuel was sleeping in the Temple near the Ark, the Lord called out, "Samuel! Samuel!"
>
> "Yes?" Samuel replied. "What is it?" He jumped up and ran to Eli. "Here I am. What do you want?" he asked.
>
> "I didn't call you," Eli said. "Go on back to bed." So he did. Then the Lord called again, "Samuel!" And again Samuel jumped up and ran to Eli.
>
> "Yes?" he asked. "What do you need?"
>
> "No, I didn't call you, my son," Eli said. "Go back to bed."
>
> (Samuel had never had a message from Jehovah before.)
>
> So now the Lord called the third time, and once more Samuel jumped up and ran to Eli.
>
> "Yes?" he asked. "What do you need?"
>
> Then Eli realized it was the Lord who had spoken

to the child. So he said to Samuel, "Go and lie down again, and if he calls again, say, 'Yes, Lord, I'm listening.'" So Samuel went back to bed.

And the Lord came and called as before, "Samuel! Samuel!"

And Samuel replied, "Yes, I'm listening."

(1 Samuel 3: 1–10, TLB)

Once God had Samuel's attention, He went on to disclose information about some coming events.

I remember the first time I read this story. It surprised me that God had chosen to share vital information with a little boy, rather than one of the chief priests or prophets. And I remember hoping that my children would one day experience intimacy with God that enabled them to hear directly from Him, too. I still have those hopes.

I pray that, like Samuel, our children will become completely comfortable with God and sense He knows them on a first name basis.

I pray that they will have the confidence to stay on speaking terms with God no matter what kinds of mistakes they make.

I pray that their ears will be finely tuned to God's voice and eager to hear from Him. I hope many times will come when they will say, "Speak, Lord, I'm listening."

And I pray they will have hearts quick to trust and quick to obey whatever God shares with them.

Our children's future depends on their listening skills and ability to hear from God. If they have a hotline to heaven, they'll be able to endure anything on earth. If they can sense the spirit of God speaking to them on the inside, they'll be able to withstand any battle on the outside. Little Samuel had some major wars ahead of him. But he also had the assurance that his heavenly Father had spoken to him and disclosed His purposes. When all hell broke loose around him, Samuel could rest in the knowledge that God was doing what He said He would do.

Jessie went to church camp for some fun and games and spiritual growth. Mom and Dad learned an important lesson that week, too. The Spirit of God can do more in a few short moments than we as parents can accomplish in years of blood, sweat, and tears.

It's a truth worth taking home to your family. And it comes with a timeless guarantee to outlast the old Samsonites packed away in your attic.

Power Perk: A Sip of Humor

A woman holding a baby boarded a hotel shuttle. The driver looked at the infant and said, "That has got to be the ugliest baby I've ever seen."

Disgusted with the man, the woman turned up her nose and stomped to the back of the shuttle to take a seat.

The man seated next to her hadn't heard the conversation when she boarded and asked why she was so upset.

"The driver offended me!" she snapped.

"Well, that's terrible!" chimed the other passenger. "He should know better than that. His first priority should be his customer's happiness."

"You've got that right," the lady retorted. "I'm gonna go back up there and give that man a piece of my mind!"

"Good idea, lady," said the traveling companion. "Here, let me help you. I'll hold your monkey."

CHAPTER 28

Happy or Holy?

*B*ut the Counselor, the Holy Spirit, whom the Father will send in
my name, will teach you all things."

—John 14:26

One of the highlights of each month is the time I spend with my
mentor, Dr. Pamela Reeve. She is a perceptive woman, full of the
Spirit of God, who lovingly speaks penetrating truth. God moves
through this woman. When I'm with her, I'm acutely aware of
His presence. Besides that, she is a well-trained counselor who
has offered hope to broken people for many years. So we speak
the same language, even though the breadth of her knowledge
far surpasses mine.

One afternoon while I was sipping a latté, I shared some things
with her that troubled me. No major crises. Just the typical stuff
parents deal with when their kids feel hurt or disappointed.

"I wish I could apply the same professional objectivity I have
with my clients to situations with my kids," I told her. "It's so easy
for me to get hooked in by my children's heartaches."

I heard another mom state this dilemma in more extreme terms:
"When my kids are happy, I'm happy. When they're not, I'm not."

The clinical label for this is codependency.

As I listened to that mother make that statement, I thought about times when I, too, had been sucked in to a similar dynamic with my children. And I didn't like it. It's a sure way to feel crazy and out of control, especially if you have teenagers susceptible to emotional roller-coaster rides.

"So when they are upset about something that has happened, how do you respond?" my mentor asked.

"I usually listen and then try to help them problem solve," I responded. It seemed like a good answer to me. After all, isn't that what responsible, loving parents are supposed to do?

"And what is your goal in the process?" she asked.

"Well, I guess my goal is to help them fix the problem and feel better."

"And what if they don't feel better?"

I laughed and jokingly said, "Then I don't feel better." I knew my statement held a kernel of truth.

Her quiet nod caused me to think about what I had said.

Bingo! The lights turned on. I began to see how self-serving my interactions were. She went on to say that there were higher purposes at work behind my children's problems and struggles.

"Pam, God isn't as concerned about your children being happy as He is about them being holy."

Ouch!

She continued. "So what would happen if you didn't try to fix things and make your kids feel better?"

"Then they'd have to think things through and wrestle with the problems more themselves," I answered.

"Do you think God is capable of helping them in the process?"

Nailed again. I knew the right answer. But I had moments when

I acted like I didn't believe it.

I thought for a moment, then said, "I guess I'm trying to determine where the line is between responsible parenting and meddling in God's business. I hear you saying my efforts to help my children problem solve and feel better may actually be interfering with something God is trying to accomplish in them."

"Yes," she responded. "God will only allow situations and circumstances to come into your children's lives that He will ultimately use for their highest good."

After our time together, I reflected on my own spiritual growth through the years. It most certainly came as the result of enduring difficulties and pain. My loving heavenly Father didn't shield me from hardship. He allowed me to struggle. And it has been through the broken places in my life that God has chosen to touch others. Why would I assume anything different for my children? God must do a work *in* my children before He will ever be able to work *through* them. He must transform them from the inside out so they will be fit for His purposes.

Once again I saw my need to surrender my children back to the Lord and to trust Him with their lives. Sometimes I'm so slow at mastering the most important basics of the Spirit-filled life. I obviously wasn't acing this "surrender" test, even though I'd had a powerful lesson just the week before....

I was in the counseling office with a client, who, in passing mentioned that she had attended a funeral for a little boy with Down Syndrome who died of leukemia. Listening to her story triggered strong emotion in me because of Nathan's Down Syndrome. At his birth we were told he would be mentally retarded and that there was a high incidence of leukemia among those with the disorder.

Listening to my client, I did the clinical thing—I suppressed the emotion and focused on her needs. But suppressed emotion doesn't stay submerged for long. It's like trying to hold a beach ball under water. No matter what you do, it keeps popping up.

I pushed her story to the back of my mind until the next evening, when I opened a letter from a woman who had read my book *Angel Behind the Rocking Chair*. She recounted some special things about her little boy, also born with Down Syndrome. She then explained how much she missed him since he died of leukemia at the tender age of eight. His death had occurred only a month before.

Well, that did it. I was in a puddle. All the emotions of the day before and all my fears for Nathan came flooding back. I went into my bedroom, sat on the bed, had a good cry, and talked to God. I told Him about my fears and asked Him to guide me. I asked Him to help me live in the here and now and not to forecast negatively into the future. And then I said something I don't think I had ever formally said before: "God, today I choose to trust you with Nathan's life and with Nathan's death."

That bedroom chat took ten minutes, even with all my blubbering. I can't tell you everything was better afterward, but a calm stilled my heart. The fear wasn't at flood stage anymore.

Effective parenting necessitates continual dialogue with God. It requires open ears to hear what the Spirit of God is saying in the midst of the struggles we encounter. When do we need to step in? When do we need to step back? The Holy Spirit is the one with the answers. If He says step in, we had best follow His lead, regardless of whether or not it makes anyone "happy."

If we are overprotective, we may produce soft kids who are unwilling to face the pain that results in growth. I don't believe there is anything arbitrary about the circumstances and struggles that touch our families. God is the master artist who shapes us and our children with unerring precision. We need not second-guess Him or develop contingency plans.

I'm reminded of a client who told me she had been sexually abused as a child. Her son was nearing the age that her molestation began. Terrified that someone was going to abuse her little boy, she took every possible precaution to control the world around him for "safety's sake." But with the start of school came invitations to friends' homes, ball games, and other fun activities. Her anxiety soared off the charts.

Toward the end of one session, I asked her to write a letter to God about her fears, and then listen to what He might say to her. She came back the following week amazed by what had happened.

"When I was done writing my letter, God told me to get out of His way," she told me. "He said I was stifling Tommy."

I had been saying the same thing in different words. But when she heard it from the Spirit of God, it stuck. She and Tommy are much better off because she yielded to the Spirit's counsel.

If the life of the Spirit is going to spring up in our children, there will be a price to pay. There will be no gain except by loss. That's what Jesus told the disciples on the way to the cross. There's a message here for those of us who tend to be too protective, reacting to life like Peter did. Impulsively, he stepped in and tried to prevent Christ's suffering by telling Him not to go to Jerusalem. What was Jesus' response?

Jesus said: "Peter, get out of my way. Satan, get lost. You have no idea how God works." Then turning to his disciples, he elaborated: "Anyone who intends to come with me has to let me lead. You're not in the driver's seat; *I* am. Don't run from suffering; embrace it. Follow me and I'll show you how" (Matthew 16:23–24, *The Message*).

When our children suffer disappointments and loss, we rightfully grieve with them. But as we grieve, we must remember that God is in the driver's seat. He's orchestrating circumstances and situations to refine their character and make them more like Him. Will you let God take the wheel? If you'll scoot to the passenger side, you'll find a note taped on the dashboard:

TRUST ME.

I HAVE EVERYTHING UNDER CONTROL.

LOVE,

GOD

Our families will suffer disappointments and loss. But God has the bigger plan all figured out. His word to you today is: "My end is never death. It is always life."

It's the message of the cross. It's God's promise to you. Will you believe it for your children?

Koffee Klatch Questions

The following questions are designed for pooped-out parents who want to share the joys and challenges of parenting with friends over coffee. Groups of two to six trusted friends can create stimulating discussion and powerful healing. Great encouragement comes from knowing we're not alone—and from hearing how others have successfully passed through tough challenges. I encourage you to be open and honest with your friends. And at the end of your discussion times, be sure to pray for one another's needs. Remember, everything isn't up to you alone.

CHAPTER ONE: TIME FOR A REFILL
1. How has parenting chipped away at your orientation toward self?
2. What are some ways God is using your children to shape and refine your character?

CHAPTER TWO: ANGEL SIGHTINGS
1. Can you identify any walls of ice in your heart that you need the Lord to melt?
2. What is one way you can extend grace to your children today?

CHAPTER THREE: THE HOSPITAL CHAPLAIN
1. All parents experience feelings of inadequacy now and then. What triggers these feelings in you and how do you usually deal with them?
2. When we're pooped out, it's easy to get on a negative track. Switch gears and identify things you do well as a parent.

CHAPTER FOUR: WAR ZONES
1. What issues create a war zone in your family?
2. What is one small step you can take together to begin muting the battle cries?

CHAPTER FIVE: RUTS
1. Describe what was going on in your life the last time you found yourself in a rut.
2. The best prescription for the Slump Syndrome is grace. How do you plan to extend grace to yourself today?

CHAPTER SIX: BEST FRIENDS
1. Share a loss that one of your children has experienced and the ways

you tried to be supportive.
2. When and how will you help your children use their pain as a springboard for prayer?

CHAPTER SEVEN: GOD CARES ABOUT WHAT MATTERS TO US
1. The father in this story had faith that the stolen bicycle would be returned in spite of apparent circumstances. Describe a situation in your life in which you are being (or have been) challenged to have faith "against the odds."
2. What problems can you ask your family or friends to pray about with you today?

CHAPTER EIGHT: PERCOLATING PRAYERS
1. Share some examples of your own quick, short percolating prayers.
2. How is your daily experience different when the prayers are "perking"?

CHAPTER NINE: A CURE FOR FRAZZLED FAMILY SYNDROME
1. What forces are currently pulling at the fabric of your family?
2. What adjustments can you make to reconnect with the most important people in your life?

CHAPTER TEN: BIRTHDAY BLOWOUTS
1. Discuss one fear that you struggle with as a parent.
2. What insight was most relevant to you in this story?

CHAPTER ELEVEN: THE PRAYERS OF A TEN-YEAR-OLD AVAILETH MUCH
1. Talk about one your children's answers to prayer—or one from your own childhood.
2. What concrete needs will you help your children pray about today?

CHAPTER TWELVE: ACCEPTING A NEW DESTINATION
1. What is the Lord nudging you to accept rather than resist?
2. For you, what are the lovely things about being in "Holland"?

CHAPTER THIRTEEN: DOUBLE BLESSING
1. What special gifts has the Lord already deposited along your children's paths?
2. How else has the Lord been working in your children?

CHAPTER FOURTEEN: IT'S JUST A MATTER OF TIME
1. Alberto's story is a powerful reminder that in God's economy, we

don't have to be products of our past. What does this mean to you as a parent?

2. What are some ways you can plant seeds of truth in your children today?

CHAPTER FIFTEEN: TALK SHOW TALES

1. Getting beyond our pain doesn't take trying harder; it takes trust. What do you need to entrust to God today?

2. Nothing can thwart God's plans. What fear will you confront with this truth?

CHAPTER SIXTEEN: THE BATTLE BELONGS TO THE LORD

1. What current parenting issue tempts you to feel discouragement and despair?

2. What battle will you ask God to fight for you today?

CHAPTER SEVENTEEN: WHEN WE ARE WEAK, HE IS STRONG

1. How is the phrase "I don't have to be strong to be strong" relevant to you?

2. In what area of weakness will you ask God to display His strength?

CHAPTER EIGHTEEN: SURPRISE ENDINGS

1. Recount some of the ways God has been faithful to meet your needs during trying times.

2. What Scripture will you review daily during the next week to bolster your faith?

CHAPTER NINETEEN: LIE DOWN IN YOUR SOUL

1. When was the last time you stopped your routine to listen quietly to the Lord? What was the result?

2. Share about an experience when you "laid down in your soul" with one of your children. What occurred?

CHAPTER TWENTY: TROUBLEMAKERS

1. Describe a situation in which one of your children was bullied. How did you deal with it?

2. What did you learn in the process? Would you do things differently next time?

CHAPTER TWENTY-ONE: HOUSE CALL

1. In what specific area are your children vulnerable to the powers of darkness?

2. How do you plan to teach them to be wise to the schemes of the enemy?

CHAPTER TWENTY-TWO: PARENTING A PRODIGAL
1. Sharon's story revealed many insights she gleaned from the Lord. Identify one insight that was helpful to your present experience as a parent.
2. Jesus said, "If you believe, you will see." How do you plan to apply this trust this week?

CHAPTER TWENTY-THREE: CRITICS
1. Share about a time when you or one of your children were on the receiving end of a critic's cruel barbs. What was your response?
2. Children are works in progress, so all judgment is provisional. What difference does this make in the way you view and relate to your children?

CHAPTER TWENTY-FOUR: HELLO, BOBBY!
1. Gramma Williamson's motto was: "Nothing will happen today that the Lord and I can't handle together." What is your motto?
2. Has there ever been a time when you, like Gramma Williamson, decided not to be on speaking terms with God? Tell about it and how you were able to reconnect with Him.

CHAPTER TWENTY-FIVE: RESTAURANT PRAYERS
1. Share a funny or embarrassing experience you've had with one of your children.
2. How have your children creatively expressed their faith?

CHAPTER TWENTY-SIX: LETTING GO OF SECOND BEST
1. What is God nudging you to let go of today?
2. Describe a time when God gave you genuine treasure in exchange for the dime-store stuff you surrendered to Him.

CHAPTER TWENTY-SEVEN: CHURCH CAMP
1. Recount a time when the Lord gave you or one of your children guidance or direction.
2. What will you do this week to nurture your children's hotline to heaven?

CHAPTER TWENTY-EIGHT: HAPPY OR HOLY?
1. Respond to the following phrase: "There are higher purposes at work behind our children's problems."
2. What is God asking you to trust Him with today?

Notes

Power Perk: A Sip of Humor (page 20) following ch. 1
1. Edyth Draper, *Draper's Book of Quotations for the Christian World* (Wheaton, Ill.: Tyndale House, 1992), entry #3879.
2. Draper, entry #3878.

Chapter 2: Angel Sightings
1. Excerpt taken from *Angel Behind the Rocking Chair* by Pam Vredevelt (Sisters, Ore.: Multnomah, 1998), 49–50, 92–4. Used by permission.

Power Perk: A Taste of Hope (page 28) following ch. 2
1. Draper, entry #3884.
2. Oswald Chambers, *Christian Disciplines, Volume One* (Fort Washington, Penn.: Christian Literature Crusade, 1936), 44.

Power Perk: A Taste of Hope (page 39) following ch. 4
1. Draper, entry #5781.

Power Perk: A Sip of Humor (page 45) following ch. 5
1. James S. Hewitt, *Illustrations Unlimited* (Wheaton, Ill.: Tyndale House, 1988), 196–7.

Power Perk: A Taste of Hope (page 52) following ch. 6
1. Draper, entry #9285.
2. Draper, entry #8896.

Power Perk: A Sip of Humor (page 57) following ch. 7
1. Sherri Weaver, *365 Days in the Stress Lane* (Glendale Heights, Ill.: Great Quotations Publishing, 1994).

Power Perk: A Taste of Hope (page 61) following ch. 8
1. Draper, entry #6334.
2. Oswald Chambers, *Run Today's Race* (Fort Washington, Penn.: Christian Literature Crusade, 1968), 7.
3. Draper, entry #9267.

Power Perk: A Taste of Hope (page 77) following ch. 10
1. Draper, entry #587.
2. Draper, entry #606.

Chapter 12: Accepting a New Destination
1. Emily Perl Kingley, from an October 1992 "Dear Abby" column in *The Oregonian* newspaper.
2. This chapter originally appeared in *Angel Behind the Rocking Chair,* 109–14. Used by permission.

Power Perk: A Taste of Hope (page 90) following ch. 12
1. Draper, entry #5389.
2. Draper, entry #5392.
3. Draper, entry #5454.

Power Perk: A Sip of Humor (page 94) following ch. 13
1. "Campus Comedy," *Reader's Digest,* April 1999, 9. The Reader's Digest Association, Inc. New York, N.Y.
2. Draper, entry #1112.
3. Draper, entry #1101.

Power Perk: A Taste of Hope (page 103) following ch. 14
1. Draper, entry #5791.
2. Oswald Chambers, *Disciples Indeed* (Fort Washington, Penn.: Christian Literature Crusade, 1968), 22.

Power Perk: A Sip of Humor (page 112) following ch. 15
1. Allen Klein, *The Healing Power of Humor* (New York, N.Y.: Penguin Putnam, Inc., 1989), 151. This letter is used by permission of Allen Klein, author of *The Healing Power of Humor, The Courage to Laugh,* and *Quotations to Cheer You Up.*
2. Ibid., 152.

Power Perk: A Taste of Hope (page 122) following ch. 16
1. A.W. Tozer, *The Pursuit of Man* (Camp Hill, Penn.: Christian Publications, 1950), 50.
2. Draper, entry #10,693.
3. Draper, entry #9858.
4. Draper, entry #9854.

Power Perk: A Taste of Hope (page 136) following ch. 18
1. Chambers, *Run Today's Race,* 89.
2. Draper, entry #5461.
3. Draper, entry #493.

Power Perk: A Sip of Humor (page 142) following ch. 19
1. Allen Klein, *The Healing Power of Humor.* These quotations are adapted and

used with permission of Allen Klein, author of *The Healing Power of Humor, The Courage to Laugh,* and *Quotations to Cheer You Up.*

Power Perk: A Taste of Hope (page 145) following ch. 20
1. Draper, entry #185.
2. Draper, entry #8907.

Power Perk: A Taste of Hope (page 160) following ch. 22
1. Draper, entry #10,867.
2. Chambers, *Christian Disciplines, Volume One,* 61.

Power Perk: A Sip of Humor (page 166) following ch. 23
1. Draper, entry #1127.
2. Draper, entry # 1136.
3. Allen Klein, *The Healing Power of Humor* (New York, N.Y.: Penguin Putnam, Inc. 1989), 13. Allen Klein is also the author of *The Courage to Laugh* and *Quotations to Cheer You Up.*

Power Perk: A Taste of Hope (page 174) following ch. 24
1. Draper, entry #8909.

Chapter 25: Restaurant Prayers
1. Story used by permission of Kim Kane.

Power Perk: A Sip of Humor (page 177) following ch. 25
1. Ellen Kirkpatrick, "Laughter, the Best Medicine," *Reader's Digest,* April 1998, 72. The Reader's Digest Association, Inc., New York, N.Y.
2. Amanda Parker, "Laughter, the Best Medicine," *Reader's Digest,* September 1998, 110. The Reader's Digest Association, Inc., New York, N.Y.

Chapter 26: Letting Go of Second Best
1. Alice Gray, "The Treasure," *More Stories for the Heart* (Sisters, Ore.: Multnomah Publishers, 1997), 147. Used by permission.

Power Perk: A Taste of Hope (page 182) following ch. 26
1. Oswald Chambers, *Disciples Indeed* (Fort Washington, Penn.: Christian Literature Crusade, 1955), 20.
2. A. W. Tozer, *Born after Midnight* (Camp Hill, Penn.: Christian Publications, 1959), 96.

ANGEL BEHIND THE
ROCKING
CHAIR

Stories of Hope in
Unexpected Places

Pam Vredevelt

In these stories of hope and encouragement, share in
the blessings and heartache that come with having a
Down Syndrome child. Walk with families that
face unexpected adversities, revealing how in the
imperfections of our lives, God's perfect glory
shines through.

ISBN 1-57673-250-9

Empty Arms

Emotional Support
for Those Who
Have Suffered
Miscarriage,
Stillbirth, or
Tubal Pregnancy

Pam Vredevelt

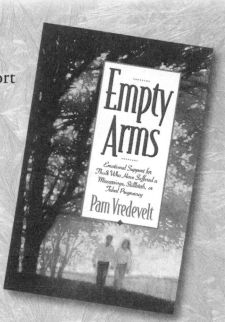

Having lost a child, Pam Vredevelt writes with compassionate insight on the emotional turmoil that can so often accompany loss. Feelings of grief, guilt, and anger, as well as the spiritual battles that women and families face, are sensitively handled with biblical hope and comfort.

ISBN 0-88070-810-7

OTHER BOOKS BY
PAM VREDEVELT

Angel Behind the Rocking Chair: Stories of Hope in Unexpected Places

Empty Arms: Emotional Support for Those Who Have Suffered Miscarriage, Stillbirth, or Tubal Pregnancy.

Mothers and Sons: Raising Boys to Be Men (with Jean Lush)

Women and Stress (with Jean Lush)

The Thin Disguise: Understanding and Overcoming Anorexia and Bulimia (with Dr. Frank Minirth, Dr. Debra Newman, and Harry Beverly)

To schedule Pam Vredevelt for conference speaking, you may write:

Pam Vredevelt (Conference)
P.O. Box 1093
Gresham, OR 97030